THE Ultimate SASHIKO SOURCEBOOK

THE Ultimate SASHIKO SOURCEBOOK

Susan Briscoe

D&C
David and Charles

For Mayor Kiichiro Onedira and the
people of Yuza-machi, Yamagata
Prefecture, Japan – thank you
for a wonderful year!

A DAVID & CHARLES BOOK

David & Charles is an imprint of F&W Media International, Ltd
Brunel House, Forde Close, Newton Abbot, TQ12 4PU, UK

F&W Media International, Ltd is a subsidiary of F+W Media, Inc
10151 Carver Road, Suite #200, Blue Ash, OH 45242, USA

First published in the UK in 2005
Reprinted in 2006, 2008, 2009, 2010, 2011, 2012, 2013

A catalogue record for this book is available from the British Library.

ISBN-13: 978-0-7153-1847-8
ISBN-10: 0-7153-1847-0

Printed in Singapore by KHL Printing Co. Pte Ltd
for David & Charles
Brunel House, Forde Close, Newton Abbot   TQ12 4PU, UK

Executive editor   Cheryl Brown
Desk editor   Ame Verso
Project editor   Lin Clements
Art editor   Prudence Rogers
Book designer   Sarah Underhill
Production controller   Jennifer Campbell

Photography by Karl Adamson, Kim Sayer, Johnny Bouchier
and Ginette Chapman

F+W Media publishes high quality books on a wide range of subjects.
For more great book ideas visit:
www.stitchcraftcreate.co.uk

(Title page): A sashiko sampler quilt bordered with
striped *tsumugi* cotton, featuring the 60 dark blue
moyōzashi sashiko patterns described in the Stitch
Library on pages 58–91.

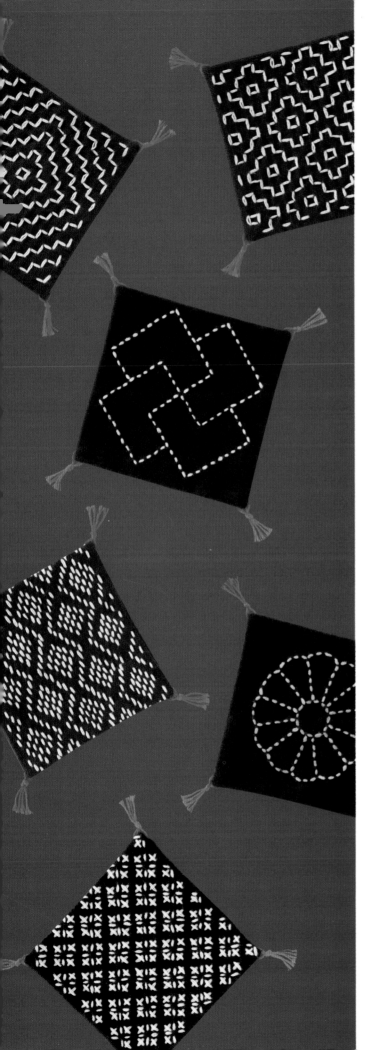

CONTENTS

INTRODUCTION

Sashiko is the magical country stitching of northern Japan. Pronounced 'sash(i)ko' (the 'i' is almost silent), it means 'little stab' or 'little pierce', an accurate description of the stitching action. Originally invented for warmth and thrifty recycling, strengthening work clothes and household goods, sashiko combines country style with intricate designs – all made with simple running stitch.

Handed down from mother to daughter, from hand to hand, in farming and fishing communities, practical and decorative sashiko created a unique style. White running stitches on indigo blue recall snow falling around the old farmhouses, while inside, women stitched beside the *irori* hearth, conjuring patterns from thread and cloth.

Most old sashiko has all-over designs of varying complexity, adapted from popular patterns. Mastering these patterns is the key to really understanding sashiko – it's not just stitching Japanese designs in outline! Sashiko sometimes includes motifs or a *kamon* (family crest) or has larger pictorial elements worked in running stitch.

I first saw sashiko stitching in 1991 in Yuza-machi in the western Shonai district of Yamagata Prefecture, Japan (a Prefecture is like a large county). I was given two pieces – a business card holder and a small mat. I was fascinated but, as a busy English teacher, I didn't have time to learn how to stitch sashiko properly. When I returned for the millennium New Year celebrations I wanted to learn.

Mayor Ken Onedira introduced me to local sashiko teacher Chie Ikeda, who taught me to sew *hitomezashi*, the small stitch patterns traditional to Shonai. My friends took me to see many inspiring works, old and new. My former neighbour, Reiko Domon, was also stitching sashiko and teaching the local quilt group. Old and new friendships finally led to the 'Magic of Sashiko' exhibition at the inaugural Festival of Quilts in Birmingham, England in 2003. Chie, Reiko and seven sashiko experts made the trip and we taught more than 150 visitors over four days, proving that stitching is a universal language. Sashiko was described as 'fascinating', 'therapeutic', 'relaxing' and even 'addictive'!

Nowadays, we don't have to be thrifty to stitch sashiko. The great variety of traditional patterns will inspire your creativity – there are over 100 patterns in this book. The book starts with a brief but fascinating history of sashiko. This is followed by a section describing everything you need to know to get started – the materials and equipment needed, how to mark designs and work the sashiko stitches. There is then a selection of easy projects to whet your appetite. Favourite traditional patterns appear in the extensive Pattern Library beginning on page 58 and, for the first time in an English-language publication, the dense *hitomezashi* patterns stitched in Shonai (pages 96–109). The projects and the patterns in the library start with the easiest, so you can work your way through them to become a real sashiko expert. 'Magic of Sashiko' exhibition highlights are included in the Inspiration Gallery beginning on page 110.

As a sashiko teacher in the United Kingdom, I have been asked many questions. I hope this book will give you the answers, with much pleasurable stitching along the way. Reflect the spirit of rural life with sashiko's classic combinations of indigo and white or echo the colours of the landscape in your creations as you capture the magic of sashiko in your work.

above: The 'Magic of Sashiko' team at the Festival of Quilts, England 2003. The large panel behind us is called '*Noshi*' by Keiko Hori, 1988 (*see picture opposite*) and the long narrow panel in the background is Shonai Sashiko Sampler by Cheiko Hori – all 13 yards of it! (See also Inspiration Gallery, page 113.)

1988·10 恵

above: '*Noshi*' wall hanging by Keiko Hori, featuring patterns traditional to Yuza-machi. All the thread is creamy white, the illusion of colour created entirely by the varying density of the patterns. From left to right, below the bundle centre are: *jūjizashi, sanjū kakinohanazashi, kusari jūjizashi, asanoha, kakinohanazashi* and *sorobanzashi* (pages 97, 101, 98, 72, 100 and 109). The appliqué was made with pieces of antique cloth from Keiko's collection before the sashiko was stitched, producing subtle colour accents. Old sashiko was patched from the back before stitching – the appliqué echoes and develops this tradition. See page 94 for more about *noshi*.

A SASHIKO HISTORY

The origins of sashiko stitching are lost in the mists of time. There are no written records of its real beginnings, no original surviving piece of work that can be conclusively dated or attributed to an individual or group. Born of necessity, sashiko was used and worn out, so very little early work remains. Decorative sashiko must have begun as someone repaired clothing, sewing *tsukuroi sashi* (darning sashiko), economically using undyed thread on dark indigo cloth and realizing the decorative possibilities in the stitches.

right and detail above: Late 19th-century man's *nogi* (work coat) from Yuza-machi, Yamagata Prefecture showing *raimon* (spiral) through two layers of indigo cotton. Work clothes were cut from old kimono.

Япония.—Le Japon. No 3.
Лавка.

above: Second-hand clothes shop, c.1900. Lengths of striped and checked fabric are displayed in the centre, with children's kimono and jackets on either side.

Sashiko evolved as a rural domestic craft in Japan during the Edo era (1615–1868), a time of increasing prosperity and peace after more than a hundred years of civil war. It made cloth stronger, improved its thermal qualities and recycled worn-out textiles – important at a time when all fibres were hand spun, hand woven and hand dyed in labour-intensive processes, from linen, hemp, ramie and other bast fibres. Fabric was remade into work wear, then into bags and aprons and finally into cleaning cloths, all with sashiko. By the Meiji era (1868–1912), sashiko was established as winter work in northern farming communities, when heavy snowfall restricted outside activities. Hand sewing was vital to a rural domestic economy and skill in sashiko was essential for a young girl wanting to make a good marriage. Girls and young women attended village needlework schools during the winter, when farm work was slack, where sashiko was passed down from hand to hand. Learning sashiko helped to instil values of patience and perseverance – essential qualities for a farmer's wife.

above and left: In Japan, inspirations for sashiko are all around – work clothes drying against *minka* (farmhouse) walls; a farmhouse with *irori* hearth and latticed *shoji* screens; rice in striped rows – all near Yuza-machi, Yamagata Prefecture.

above and left: *Tsukuroi sashi* (darning sashiko) is shown in these two early 20th-century *noragi* (work coats) from Tohoku, heavily patched inside and out. *Tsukuroi sashi* was stitched by men and women. The darker indigo jacket was darned after it was made but the other is made from a patchwork of scraps with each section heavily stitched with plain sashiko in indigo thread before making up. Like patchwork quilts, antique sashiko may have fabric much older than the stitching.

below: Old country clothes – women planting rice and returning from the fields.

Reusing textiles has a long tradition in Japan, for economic and spiritual reasons. A *funzō-e kesa* (Buddhist priest's mantle) in the Shōsōin, the imperial repository at Nara in central Japan, is an early example. It belonged to Emperor Shōmu who abdicated in AD749 to become a monk. It is made from scraps of plain weave silk, resembling raw edge appliqué, with parallel lines of running stitch in purple silk thread. Unlike commoners' sashiko, here the old cloth is meant to be seen. *Funzō-e* made from rags and discarded fabrics were a symbol of humility and the vow of poverty. Making *kesa* was an act of devotion and prayers were recited while working.

Urban fire-fighters' protective clothing of the Edo period also used plain sashiko. Fire-fighting teams would pull down timber buildings to create a fire break rather than quench the blaze with water and sashiko gave some protection from falling tiles and timber. *Hanten* (half wear) jackets and helmets, made from many layers of cloth, were doused with water before use. Decorative, painted or dyed *hanten* linings resembled traditional tattoos. They were displayed by turning the *hanten* inside out after extinguishing a fire or during festival parades.

Sashiko uses

Household textiles – *kotatsugake* (table cover), *zabuton* (floor cushion), thin *kakebuton* (futon quilt), *futongawa* (futon cover), *furoshiki* (wrapping cloth), *noren* (door curtain), *kinchaku* (drawstring bag), *komebukuro* (rice bag) and *fukin* (cleaning cloth – see below).

Clothing – *donza*, *noragi* and *nogi* (work jackets), *hanten* (short jacket), *sodenashi* ('without sleeves' waistcoat), *sorihikihappi* (sled-hauling waistcoat), *maekake* ('front wear' apron), *tekkou* (hand protector), *kyahan* (gaiter), *tabi* (sock), *agudokake* or *akutogake* (heel protector, worn with snow boots), *warajikake* (toe protector) and *kōgake* (instep protector, for straw sandals).

below: Traditional bedding or futon – *shikibuton* for a mattress and *kakebuton* as a winter cover. *Futongawa* (futon covers) and lightweight *kakebuton* were sometimes made with sashiko. Note the *yogi*, a thickly padded quilt shaped like a gigantic kimono, and the *zabuton* (floor cushion).

above: Unused vintage *fukin* (cleaning cloths) with simple sashiko.

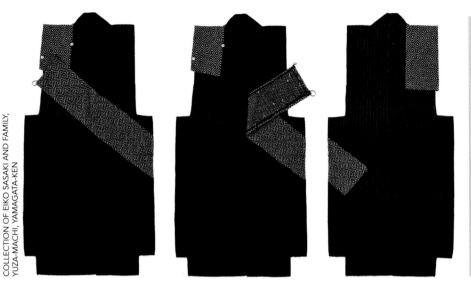

left: Late Meiji Era Shōnai sashiko *sorihikihappi* (sled-hauling waistcoat), with protective shoulder patch and front band in *kakinohanazashi* (persimmon flower stitch). The extra band, fastened with buttons, and patch protected the garment from wear by the sled strap. Women made a new *sorihikihappi* for their husbands at New Year, with an elaborate design showing the family's status. Decorative sashiko like this was made for best. It is rare for us to know the identity of the stitcher – this was made by the Sasaki family's great grandmother.

The sashiko stitch

Old sashiko combines fabric in two or three layers, with the best cloth on the top, and even the most complicated patterns are made with simple running stitch. Today, it may have only one layer or include polyester or cotton quilt wadding (batting). Layers of old, worn fabric were formerly used instead of wadding, so vintage sashiko is much flatter than traditional Western quilts. The stitches themselves create the textured pattern, sitting on the fabric surface. The patterns in this book fall into two main groups – *moyōzashi* (pattern sashiko) and *hitomezashi* (one stitch sashiko) – and can be used together on the same project to great effect. Many *hitomezashi* patterns have horizontal or vertical stitches only, which looks like pattern darning, although modern *hitomezashi* is not worked as a counted thread technique. *Kogin* and *Nanbu hishizashi* (top of page 13) are thought to have evolved from this kind of sashiko.

Moyōzashi (pattern sashiko) has curved or straight lines of running stitch which change direction to make larger patterns but the stitches do not cross. The threads are not counted, although the stitches may be. Continuous lines and doubled thread give sashiko strength and warmth.

Hitomezashi (one stitch sashiko) This is typical of Shōnai in Yamagata Prefecture and is worked as a grid of straight lines, where stitches meet or cross to make the design. Some of the patterns resemble blackwork embroidery or Indian kantha quilting. Very dense *hitomezashi* patterns may use only one thread.

left: Late 19th century fishermen wearing *donza* (long work coats) heavily sashiko stitched for warmth and wear.

below: Fishing boats on the Inland Sea, Awaji Island. Stylized wave, mist and net patterns on sashiko clothes reflected the environment and the importance of the sea's bounty for coastal communities.

below: Peasant woman weaving checked cotton at home. The *takabata* (high loom) replaced the ancient *izaribata* back strap looms in rural homes during the 19th century. Cloth woven on the *izaribata* is only as wide as the weaver's body, hence the narrow width of traditional Japanese cloth.

STEREO-VIEW PHOTOGRAPH 1904, AUTHOR'S COLLECTION

below: Three generations of women hand spinning on the veranda. Note the *kagome* bamboo baskets in the foreground (see pages 83 and 100 for *kagome* sashiko patterns).

Regional sashiko traditions

Sashiko may have evolved independently in various parts of Japan or it may have originated in one area and spread from there. Design similarities between different regions suggest sashiko was spread by trade. It is associated with the Japan Sea coast and the north, where it was used as farmer's clothing. In the south it was worn by fishermen only. Edo era Shōnai sashiko survives and there are 19th-century examples from many other areas along the Japan Sea trade route.

The map opposite shows the *Kitamaebune* coastal trading route, which during the Edo era linked the Kansai region (around Kyoto) with the north-western coast of Tohoku via the Inland Sea and the Sea of Japan. Ships travelled the route yearly, leaving Osaka and trading all along the coast, up to Hokkaido. The trade brought cotton to the far north, as raw fibre, thread and fabric (old and new). It played an important role in the distribution of ideas, which must have included sashiko designs.

Shōnai sashiko has a vast range of patterns, mostly *hitomezashi*. This prosperous agricultural region was a meeting point of Edo, *Kamigata* and Tohoku cultures and design. *Kakurezashi* (hidden sashiko), over-dyed with indigo so the pattern is revealed as it fades, and *chirimenzashi* (crêpe sashiko), where straight stitch lines were deliberately puckered up to resemble crêpe, were also made.

Blue and white, white and blue

Traditional sashiko was usually indigo and white. This characteristic look was a response to Edo era sumptuary laws which prohibited the lower classes from wearing brightly coloured clothing and large patterns. Commoners could use indigo, so old indigo cloth was available in the home. The colour is still appreciated for its beauty. *Polygonum tinctorium*, Japanese indigo, can be grown to make an affordable dye. Fabric woven at home and recycled fabrics were sent to skilled professionals for dyeing. Synthetic indigo was introduced in the late 19th century and consequently there are few traditional dye shops in Japan today.

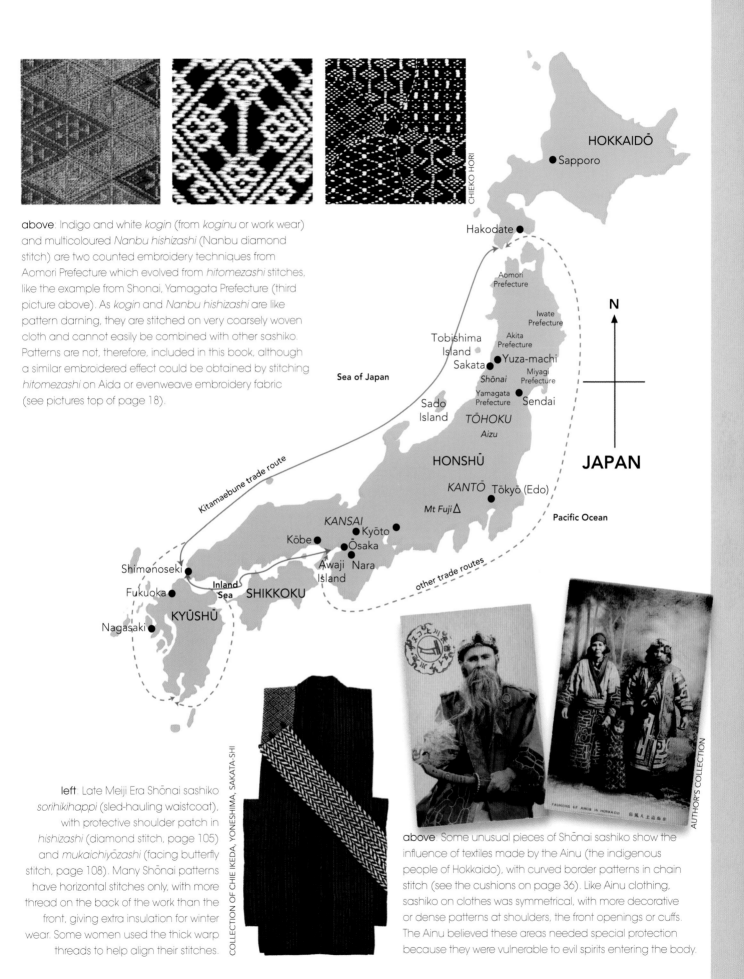

above: Indigo and white *kogin* (from *koginu* or work wear) and multicoloured *Nanbu hishizashi* (Nanbu diamond stitch) are two counted embroidery techniques from Aomori Prefecture which evolved from *hitomezashi* stitches, like the example from Shonai, Yamagata Prefecture (third picture above). As *kogin* and *Nanbu hishizashi* are like pattern darning, they are stitched on very coarsely woven cloth and cannot easily be combined with other sashiko. Patterns are not, therefore, included in this book, although a similar embroidered effect could be obtained by stitching *hitomezashi* on Aida or evenweave embroidery fabric (see pictures top of page 18).

CHIEKO HORI

HOKKAIDŌ

● Sapporo

Hakodate ●

Aomori
Prefecture

Iwate
Prefecture

Akita
Prefecture

N

Tobishima
Island

● Yuza-machi

Sakata ●

Miyagi
Prefecture

Shōnai

Sea of Japan

Yamagata
Prefecture

● Sendai

Sado
Island

TŌHOKU

Aizu

HONSHŪ

JAPAN

KANTŌ   ● Tōkyō (Edo)

Mt Fuji △

Pacific Ocean

Kitamaebune trade route

KANSAI

● Kyōto

Kōbe ●

● Ōsaka

other trade routes

Shimonoseki ●

Awaji   Nara
Island

Fukuoka ●

**Inland
Sea**   **SHIKKOKU**

KYŪSHŪ

Nagasaki ●

left: Late Meiji Era Shōnai sashiko *sorihikihappi* (sled-hauling waistcoat), with protective shoulder patch in *hishizashi* (diamond stitch, page 105) and *mukaichiyōzashi* (facing butterfly stitch, page 108). Many Shōnai patterns have horizontal stitches only, with more thread on the back of the work than the front, giving extra insulation for winter wear. Some women used the thick warp threads to help align their stitches.

COLLECTION OF CHIE IKEDA, YONESHIMA, SAKATA-SHI

above: Some unusual pieces of Shōnai sashiko show the influence of textiles made by the Ainu (the indigenous people of Hokkaido), with curved border patterns in chain stitch (see the cushions on page 36). Like Ainu clothing, sashiko on clothes was symmetrical, with more decorative or dense patterns at shoulders, the front openings or cuffs. The Ainu believed these areas needed special protection because they were vulnerable to evil spirits entering the body.

AUTHOR'S COLLECTION

Indigo and white colour combinations give sashiko a strong tonal contrast. Migration of indigo from fabric to thread often tinted old sashiko stitching pale ice blue. Blue on blue was also common. Indigo strengthens fibres and the residual smell of fermented indigo and ammonia in the dye was believed to repel snakes and insects.

Cotton has been grown commercially in Japan since the 1600s, first as a luxury fibre, and by the early 19th century it was widely cultivated south of the Aizu region. Patterned cotton fabrics were used for sashiko in some areas. *Kasuri* (ikat), *katazome* (stencilled) or *shibori* (tie-dyed) cloth were popular in Aomori Prefecture, while *shima* (striped) cotton was used for fishermen's coats in Iwate and Miyagi Prefectures on the Pacific coast.

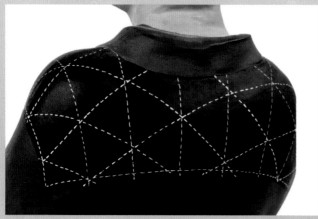

above: Sashiko *hanten* jackets typify fishermen's traditional clothes, as shown by this ceramic Hakata *ningyo* (doll) figurine, made in Kyushu, Japan in the 1950s. A simple pattern of triangles, like the first step of *asanoha* (hemp leaf, page 72), is painted stitch-by-stitch across the jacket's shoulders. Hakata *ningyo* are noted for their detailed and acurate costume decoration. Even without his net, this fisherman's profession can be identified by his clothing.

Stitches like snow

In Shōnai, sashiko is said to represent snow on the ground. The stitches do not represent rice grains, although *moyōzashi* stitches resemble them. By official order during the Edo era, farmers in Shōnai could only wear blue or grey colours with patterns no larger than a grain of rice or with stripes no thicker than a straw. This could be the origin of the idea that sashiko stitches must resemble grains of rice. *Komezashi* (rice stitch, page 97, shown right) is so called because it looks like the kanji character for rice.

A treasury of patterns

Since the 18th century, sashiko patterns have been adapted from popular designs, including those of other textiles, auspicious patterns and designs derived from Buddhist motifs. As part of the reforms of the Meji Restoration (1868), old sumptuary laws were repealed. Commoners could now wear large, colourful patterns and tastes changed. Many larger sashiko patterns date from the Taisho era (1912–26), when traditional sashiko reached its peak. Designs were adapted from textiles, paper, ceramics, marquetry and architectural details. Pattern books for textiles had been published since the Edo period and these influenced sashiko patterns too.

above: Woven patterns could be used to help align sashiko stitches or be completely disregarded, as in this Taisho era *furoshiki* (wrapping cloth) from Shikkoku. Tie it to show the corner fan or the variation on *shippō tsunagi* (page 64). *Shima* (checks) are less common than stripes.

Auspicious designs

Stitching fabric, especially for your family, creates something special in all cultures (just think of the reasons for making a quilt). In Japan, *takonomakura* (five-pointed cross) protected Kyushu fishermen from shipwreck while a pentagonal star and five criss-crossed lines were talismans for female divers in Mie Prefecture. Three, five and seven are lucky numbers, often reflected in sashiko designs. Zigzag patterns were considered protective, as evil spirits cannot follow the zigzag lines (the same belief behind zigzag bridges in Japanese gardens), and diamond points also kept evil away. In Shōnai, certain patterns are stitched to bring prosperity, so *komezashi* (rice stitch) would be appropriate for a farmer and *urokozashi* (fish scale stitch) for a fisherman. Paired or double motifs are associated with weddings. See the Pattern Library pages 58–109 for more information.

Sashiko decline and revival

By the 1950s, increased prosperity and the introduction of man-made fibres began to change the way country people dressed, and sashiko declined. Old, worn sashiko garments were not always valued and many were thrown away. Modern redevelopment has taken a toll on the old *kura* (family storehouses) where sashiko was stored, as have fires and earthquakes. Fortunately, the respect for old cloth led some people to carefully preserve old sashiko and other textiles, which are now prized by museums and collectors as examples of *mingei* (folk art). A sashiko revival began in the 1970s, parallel to the rise in Western quilting in Japan. As the role of sashiko as a frugal necessity has disappeared, people are appreciating stitching sashiko for its creative, relaxing and even therapeutic qualities. In the 21st century, sashiko continues to evolve.

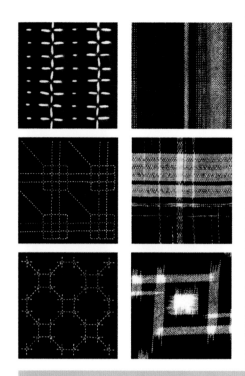

above: *Hanashijūshi* (flower cross, page 100), *koshi tsunagi* (linked check, page 80) and *igeta ni hakkaku tsunagi* (special linked well curb, page 79) reflect stripe, check and *kasuri* ikat textiles respectively. These popular patterns were more complex to weave than plain indigo but sashiko gave a similar efffect.

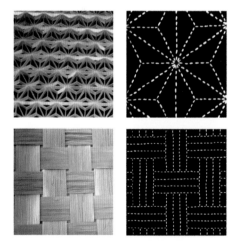

above: Patterns used for sashiko inspired by architectural and interior design details include, *asanoha* (hemp leaf, page 72) and *ishidatami* (paving block, page 77), as shown in an antique screen panel over a doorway and a modern ceiling woven from thin strips of wood. *Ishidatami* is an ancient paving pattern.

left: Popular early 20th-century patterns. The woman on the right wears a red *tasuki* cord on her shoulders to keep her kimono sleeves out of the way while resting her bucket on the *igeta* (well curb, see sashiko pattern on page 79). The crouching woman's kimono is stencilled with *kakuyose* (intersecting square corners, see pattern on page 78).

EARLY 20TH-CENTURY POSTCARD, AUTHOR'S COLLECTION

GETTING STARTED

This section describes the tools, equipment and materials you will need for sashiko stitching. Beginning on page 22 are marking and stitching techniques, information on drawing patterns, using grids, transferring designs to fabric, starting to stitch and finishing off – everything you need to help you create beautiful sashiko easily, right from the start.

EQUIPMENT AND MATERIALS

Stitching sashiko requires very few tools and materials. You will need a basic sewing and marking kit (see below) – inexpensive items you probably have in your sewing basket already. A quilting frame or hoop is not used in sashiko. Because sashiko needs little equipment, it can be stored in a bag, like one of the drawstring bags on page 48, so your sashiko things are always to hand, ready to be taken out at a moment's notice.

Sewing and marking kit

- Sashiko needles (various sizes)
- Small embroidery scissors
- Dressmaking scissors
- Quilting pins
- Thimble (optional)
- Tacking (basting) thread
- Sewing thread to match your fabrics
- Sewing sharps
- Pincushion or needle case
- Iron
- Marking tools (see right and page 19)
- Ruler

Basic equipment

Marking tools You will need an assortment of these, including markers for dark and light fabrics, rulers and templates for marking curves. Marking tools are described in more detail on page 19 and using them on page 22.

Cutting mat and quilter's ruler These are useful for precision marking. You might also prefer to cut out your fabrics with a rotary cutter.

Japanese embroidery scissors (pictured left) These are not essential, but make sewing sashiko feel very authentic!

Kakehari (pictured below) This is a sewing clamp sold as a 'third hand' or 'sewing bird'. It is useful for keeping your work under tension when sewing straight lines.

Thimble Thimbles are optional: some stitchers like them, others do without. The traditional Japanese 'ring' thimble (pictured below) is worn on the second joint of the middle finger of the sewing hand with the eye end of a short needle resting against it. A 'coin' thimble, (pictured below) with a dimpled disk to push the needle, is used with longer needles.

Sewing machine Although old sashiko items were made completely by hand, a sewing machine with zigzag and straight stitches is useful for making up projects. Fabrics suitable for sashiko tend to fray, so zigzag the edges before you begin hand stitching. If you want to finish cushions with zips, you will need a zipper foot for the machine.

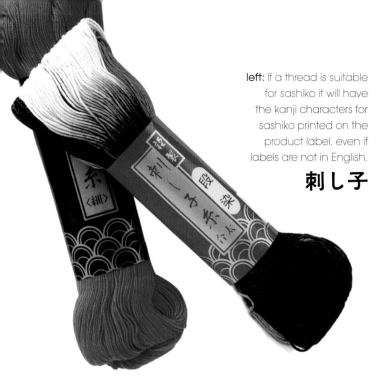

left: If a thread is suitable for sashiko it will have the kanji characters for sashiko printed on the product label, even if labels are not in English.

刺し子

Thread

Ordinary fabric and needles were originally used for sashiko but the thread was specially spun. Modern sashiko thread has a looser twist than many embroidery threads and is made from long, staple cotton so it is very hardwearing and strong – don't try breaking it with your fingers! Various brands are sold worldwide, in large skeins and several weights – fine, medium and thick – with colours and variegated effects as well as white, cream and indigo. The exact thickness and shade varies between manufacturers, so use the same brand throughout a project. If you cannot obtain real sashiko thread, cotton à broder makes a reasonable, if expensive, substitute. Cotton perlé does not look or behave like sashiko thread, although it can add interesting colour accents. Thread made for sashiko will give you the best results as a beginner and you can experiment to find other suitable threads later on, once you know what sashiko thread looks and feels like. See page 23 for using sashiko thread.

Needles

Sashiko needles are very sharp and, compared with Western sewing needles, quite thick and rigid in relation to their length. Very long needles will help keep your stitching lines straight and speed up sewing, once you are used to them. If you hand quilt with 'Betweens' (special short quilting needles), you may find the smaller sashiko needles easier to manage at first, although the smallest are only suitable for fine sashiko thread. If sashiko needles are unavailable, try using embroidery crewels or larger darning needles instead.

Match your thread and fabric weight to a suitable sashiko needle (shown right). As a rule, thinner threads and smaller needles will work with slightly heavier fabrics but it will be difficult to stitch a thick sashiko thread with a large needle through finer fabrics. If sashiko feels like hard work, change to a finer thread and needle or to a fabric with a lower thread count.

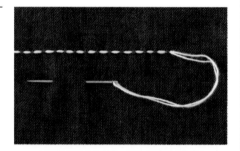

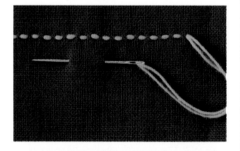

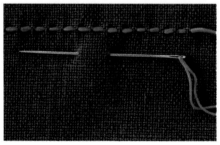

top: Fine sashiko thread and *tsumugi* cotton fabric;
middle: Medium sashiko thread and reproduction sashiko cotton;
bottom: Thick sashiko thread and prairie cloth (all shown slightly smaller than life size).

right: Some hand-dyed embroidery threads are suitable for sashiko.

Fabrics

Most modern households are unlikely to have a steady supply of old indigo cloth for recycling. Machine-made copies of these old hand-woven fabrics are specially made for sashiko, in indigo and other shades (see Suppliers, page 126). Using more colours in sashiko is a fairly recent development and fabric and threads often echo natural dyes. Choose plain weaves and natural fibres with a lower thread count (the number of threads to the inch), slightly thicker than you might normally choose for quilting. Some quilting and craft fabrics, such as prairie cloth and cotton flannel, are pleasant to stitch and look authentic. Practise grid-based *hitomezashi* (one stitch sashiko, see page 96) on checked fabrics or use woven stripes to line up pattern elements. Asian fabrics made for household textiles are an excellent source of thicker cottons and dress-making fabrics can be used too. Sashiko was originally stitched on cotton, linen, hemp and other plant

above: This experiment by Deborah Gordon, one of my sashiko students, combines *hitomezashi* as counted embroidery with couching and appliqué on 16-count Aida fabric. *Kakinohanazashi* (persimmon flower stitch, page 100) and *zenizashi* (coin stitch, page 99) are two *hitomezashi* stitches that adapt well to counted embroidery.

fibres, so experiment! For a hint of luxury, I used raw silk for the sampler cushions on page 36.

If the fabric is right but the colour isn't what you want, you can always dye it – imitation indigo dyes (sold for re-dyeing jeans) are easy to use in the washing machine, following the instructions supplied. Internet and mail-order shopping means it is easier than ever to buy materials suitable for sashiko (see Suppliers).

above: This drawstring bag by Wendy Young, one of my students, has been stitched with *asanoha* (hemp leaf, page 72). Indian cotton ikat fabrics make good substitutes for old Japanese *kasuri*.

above, from top: Old cotton *katazome* (stencil-dyed), two *kasuri* ikats, a woven stripe and eight indigo cottons. Skilled hand-dyers used natural indigo to create many shades of blue.

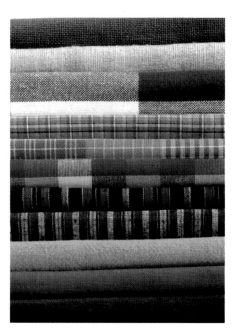

above, from top: New fabrics, including American prairie cloth, Thai raw silk, Indian cotton, three German checked cottons, two Japanese striped cotton *tsumugi* and three colours of reproduction sashiko cotton.

Wadding (batting)

If your project requires wadding (batting), mark your sashiko design before tacking (basting) the top, wadding and backing together. Vintage sashiko used two or more layers of old cloth, with the best cloth on top. Today, sashiko is made with two or three layers of cloth or with modern wadding or as embroidery, through one layer only. Here are some points to bear in mind when using wadding or fabric layers:

- If you use quilt wadding, you will also need backing fabric whereas an extra fabric layer does not need extra backing.

- If you are using dark fabric, remember that white polyester wadding might 'beard' through and spoil your work.

- The new black waddings, available in polyester or cotton and polyester mixtures, are excellent for sashiko (see Suppliers page 126).

- Cotton wadding can be dyed dark blue in the washing machine. It absorbs a lot of dye so use the actual weight of the fabric as a guide.

- Select thin cotton wadding (sold as 'request' weight) for a similar look to several layers of old cloth, or use layers of butter muslin.

- Old linen blouses, tea towels and flannel sheets can be recycled as wadding/backing, dyed darker as necessary.

- Test a small sample of your chosen wadding/backing combination by stitching a few rows of sashiko – if it is very hard to get the needle through, use thinner wadding or a more loosely woven backing fabric.

- Tightly woven calico is not a good choice for backing sashiko!

Fabric markers

Before you tack (baste) your fabric layers together, you will need to mark your chosen sashiko pattern on the fabric – see page 22 for the various techniques. There are many marker options for the modern sashiko stitcher and some are shown below. Experiment to find your favourite.

Hera This is a traditional Japanese sewing marker made of bone or plastic which scores and polishes a line on the cloth. It shows up well on very dark fabrics and the line washes out. Put a cutting mat or card-board under your fabric when marking or you will score your table!

Air-erasable marking pen (white) This felt-tip pen marks white and fades on exposure to air. The marks should last for 48 hours but can fade sooner, so it is only useful for small projects. Washing the chemical residue out when work is complete is highly recommended.

Chaco liner This is a Japanese chalk wheel that makes marks on fabric which brush off easily or wash out. A tiny wheel in the tip picks up the chalk and marks the fabric. Chalk refills are available in white, pink, yellow and blue. I find that white or yellow are best on dark fabrics.

Quilter's silver pencil This is best for light fabrics, as the marks can be difficult to see on dark or medium colours. The marks wash out or rub off.

Soapstone marker Natural soapstone in a holder can be sharpened to a fine line. When the marks are no longer required, do not iron over them but wash them out with plain water.

Soap slivers Marking dark fabrics with the edge of a piece of soap is an old quilters' trick which can be used when marking sashiko.

Tailor's chalk This is an inexpensive marker which is available in various colours. Yellow or white are best for dark fabric.

Quilter's white pencil This soft pencil is good for dark fabrics, with marks that wash out or rub off. Soft pencils will last much longer if you sharpen them with a craft knife, cutting away on either side and trimming to make a flat point.

White marking pen This pen, recently introduced, is a roller ball that makes a fine, clear white line which takes a few seconds to appear after drawing. The marks can be removed with water or heat (check brand information).

Chaco pencil This is a compressed chalk pencil that makes marks which brush off easily or wash out. It is available in the same colours as the chaco liner, above. See quilter's white pencil (far left) for sharpening advice.

BASIC TECHNIQUES

All the basic techniques you will need for sashiko embroidery are covered here – including drawing and marking patterns, tacking (basting) fabric layers together, starting and finishing work and the sashiko stitching technique.

Drawing patterns using grids

Learning how to draw the patterns is the key to making sashiko work for you. Stencils for some sashiko patterns can be bought in quilt shops but although they are easy to use, you have to fit your project to the size of the pattern on the stencil. Furthermore, only the more popular designs are available. Sheets of complete patterns to trace have similar limitations.

By starting to draw each design with a grid, the traditional *moyōzashi* (pattern sashiko) designs in the Pattern Library can be marked and stitched the size you want. If you make them on the same grid as my samples they will be a good average size, but you can easily change the dimensions for decorative effect by drawing larger or smaller starting grids. The basic grid size I used is given with each pattern sample.

Some designs can be stitched straight on to the grid, such as *sayagata* (page 90), while others need some extra marking, such as *asanoha* (page 72). Refer to the Pattern Library beginning on page 58 for full details on how to draw the patterns.

Most *hitomezashi* (one stitch sashiko) patterns are stitched back and forth on a grid without extra pattern lines, therefore little variation in the grid size is necessary. Fabric with ¼in (6mm) or ³⁄₁₆in (5mm) checks can be stitched without marking. A few of the more challenging patterns require extra marking, to help you line up your patterns rather than stitching along the lines (see individual *hitomezashi* patterns from page 96–109 for more information).

Whichever pattern you want to draw, you will need a ruler. Quilter's rulers are transparent and have extra lines parallel to the edge, so you can easily draw a grid. Some brands have yellow as well as black markings which show up well on dark fabrics. See page 22 for pattern-marking methods using graph paper or a cutting mat marked with a grid. Using an ordinary clear plastic ruler is fine.

You will also need a selection of curved templates for marking patterns with curved lines. You can make your own circle templates with a protractor and some card or template plastic (available from quilting shops). Old thread spools and even coins are useful for smaller circle templates. Don't forget all the large circle templates that are 'free' with food packaging! An oval template is necessary for only one pattern in this book, *tatewaku* (rising steam), and this is provided on page 70 for you to trace. You can buy oval template stencils at some art shops.

Imperial or metric?

Patterns can be drawn in imperial or metric measurements. I used imperial for my samples, as many quilters worldwide use this system. An imperial–metric conversion formula is given below, with some common conversions listed, right, (metric adjusted to nearest mm). Metric equivalents are given for the projects on pages 26–57.

To convert inches to centimetres: multiply measurement in inches by 2.54, e.g. 2in x 2.54 = 5.08cm

To convert centimetres to inches: multiply measurement in centimetres by 0.394, e.g. 5cm x 0.394 = 1.97in

Because a fraction of a patchwork seam is taken up by the thickness of the stitched line, it is adequate to round measurements up or down to the nearest millimetre when cutting out fabric pieces.

Neither measurement system is 100 per cent traditional in Japan – you would have to mark using the ancient *sun* and *shaku* (Japanese feet and inches). It would be difficult to mark in traditional proportions, as one sun is made up of ten bu and equals 1.193in (3.03cm) and ten sun make one shaku, 11.93in (30.3cm)! These measures were standardized in 1891 and Japan officially converted to metric in 1959. However, some traditional fabric shops and kimono makers still use them.

⅛in	(0.125in)	= 3mm
¼in	(0.25in)	= 6mm
⅜in	(0.375in)	= 1cm
½in	(0.5in)	= 1.3cm
¾in	(0.75in)	= 1.9cm
⅞in	(0.875in)	= 2cm
1in		= 2.5cm
1¼in	(1.25in)	= 3.2cm
1½in	(1.5in)	= 3.8cm
1¾in	(1.75in)	= 4.4cm
2in		= 5.1 cm
2½in	(2.5in)	= 6.4cm
3in		= 7.6cm
3½in	(3.5in)	= 8.9cm
4in		= 10.2cm
5in		= 12.7cm
6in		= 15.2cm
12in		= 30.5cm
1 yard	(36in)	= 91.44cm
1 metre		= 39.4in

Varying the grids

Many *moyōzashi* designs are based on a square grid while others require a diagonal or triangular grid (see diagram below left). If you look closely at many traditional Japanese designs with diamonds, hexagons or triangles, you will see that they are not drawn on a true isometric 60-degree grid – the

diamonds look slightly wide, the hexagons a little squashed and the triangles are not truly equilateral. To keep this look, start with a rectangular grid on a 2:1 ratio and fill in with diagonal lines (below centre). If you want an isometric grid, perhaps to integrate your sashiko with patchwork

hexagons and stars, use isometric graph paper, the 60-degree angle on a quilter's ruler or a 60/30-degree set square to create the grid (below right). There is only one pattern in this book that requires a true isometric grid – *maru bishamon* (circular bishamon, page 65).

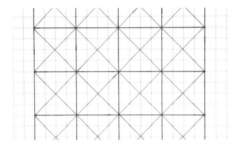
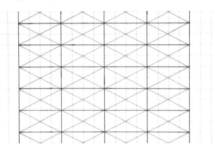
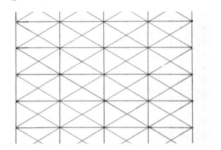

Distorting patterns

Grids are also the key to stretching patterns vertically or slanting them horizontally to give them a different look. Various *moyōzashi* patterns can be treated this way, as shown by some of the examples illustrated below. Compare *asanoha* (hemp leaf, page 72) with *kawari asanoha* (hemp leaf variation, page 73): the basic grid for the first pattern is on a rectangular 1:2 ratio; the second is on a square grid, with the rest of the pattern marked the same way as the basic pattern but following the square grid.

Jūjitsunagi (linked '10' crosses, page 75) becomes *nanamehōgan tsunagi* (diagonal linked crosses, page 75) when the same pattern is stitched on a diagonal grid rather than a square one. The two versions of *sayagata* (saya brocade pattern, page 90) are treated the same way.

I gave *higaki* (cypress fence, page 77) this treatment when I used it inside a *matsukawabishi* (pine bark diamond, page 84) outline on the door curtain project on page 44, so the pattern harmonized with the outline shape.

It's all about using the patterns in your design. For example, *shippō tsunagi* (linked seven treasures, page 64) could be elongated into elegant ovals. The framed sashiko sampler on page 26 has *asanoha* (hemp leaf, page 72) stretched to fit the frame. Learn the features of a new pattern by stitching the basic version first before embarking on your own distorted version. If you enjoy drawing perspective effects, the straight line patterns are interesting: curved line patterns would be challenging but not impossible!

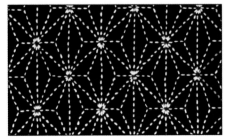
Asanoha

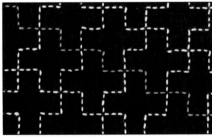
Jūjitsunagi

Sayagata

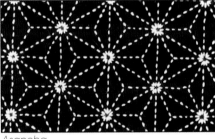
Kawari asanoha

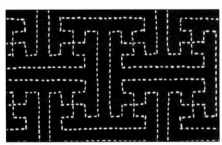
Nanamehōgan tsunagi

Sayagata variation

Transferring designs to fabric – marking methods

There are various methods for marking your sashiko pattern on to your fabric. You can mark the pattern directly on to the top fabric or draw the design on paper and transfer it. The most useful methods are described here.

Marking directly on fabric

This is my favourite method and I use it whenever possible as you can always see exactly what you are marking. There are many marking materials for dark fabrics, so try several and use your favourite (see page 19). Drawing around curved templates is easier with pencils or pens than with a block of chalk. Some marks stay on the fabric for longer than others but can also depend on factors like humidity and hand warmth. If you already have a preferred method for marking dark fabric (such as slivers of soap) use that. Always follow the manufacturer's instructions when using a new marking product – what removes one kind of mark may permanently set another.

Marking fabric with a quilter's ruler

Quilter's rulers are very accurate. Use the parallel lines on the ruler, as shown below, to mark the base grid for the pattern and mark directly on the fabric. Allow for the width of the line, especially if using tailor's chalk as the line might be up to $1/8$in (3mm) thick, so line up with the bottom of each line

or your grid might be $1^1/8$in (2.9cm) not 1in (2.5cm)! Draw the rest of the pattern with curved templates or extra diagonal lines, following the individual diagrams in the Pattern Library.

Marking fabric with a cutting mat

Use the grid on a cutting mat to mark the base grid and mark directly on the fabric. Some mats have both imperial and metric grids and you can use an ordinary ruler with the mat. The fabric will need to be smaller than the mat, so you can see the mat grid all round the edge, and the ruler should be long enough to reach across the mat.

Marking fabric using graph paper and chaco paper

Chaco paper is a kind of dressmaker's carbon paper which makes marks that wash out. It can be reused and is available in white, yellow, pink and blue. It is a good method for marking motifs like *kamon* (family crests, page 93). Not being able to see your fabric while marking can be a disadvantage as it is easy to accidentally move your fabric and spoil the transferred design.

First draw the pattern on to graph paper. Put the chaco paper face down on the fabric with the pattern on top and pin together. For smaller pieces, tape all the layers to the top of a cutting mat or some thick card. Trace along all the design lines with a ballpoint transfer tool – the end of a knitting needle or something similar. I used red ballpoint pen so lines would be clearly visible in these photographs. A dressmaker's marking wheel is useful but it will damage your cutting mat, so replace the mat with some scrap cardboard. As you trace, the pattern will be transferred to the fabric. To mark a grid quickly for *hitomezashi*, use a piece of graph or squared paper on top and draw along the lines using a ruler as a guide.

Tacking (basting) fabric layers

After you have marked your fabric with a sashiko pattern, you need to prepare your fabric for sewing if two more more layers are being used.

Begin by tacking (basting) each piece of your sashiko project to the backing and/or wadding (batting). Lay the backing fabric right side down on a flat surface, smooth out the wadding (if used) on top and lay the sashiko fabric right side up on top. Tack (baste) through all the layers to hold them together, radiating outwards from the centre. Lines of tacking up to 2in (5cm) apart are fine. If you are going to stitch sashiko on a large quilt, prepare the quilt sandwich the same way but add extra rows of tacking across the work.

Using sashiko thread

First open out the skein and remove the paper band. Look for the extra loop of thread tied around the skein and cut through *all* the threads at this point. The threads will seem very long but don't cut them – sashiko skeins are made to just the right length for using the thread. Hold the other end of the skein and loosely plait the threads to keep them tidy. Draw out individual threads from the top of the plait.

Starting and finishing sashiko stitching

Now you have marked your pattern and tacked (basted) the fabric layers together you are ready to begin stitching.

The two basic methods of starting are with or without a knot. I almost always use a knot as it is much more secure. Remember, sashiko was used for items that received hard wear and the knot-free method can eventually come undone. Old sashiko garments made from traditional narrow cloth could have the knots hidden in a seam.

Whichever method you choose to start with, first thread your needle with a single length of thread. Pull the two ends together and smooth down the length of the thread to remove excess twist. Holding the thread taut between your hands and twanging it with your thumbs is also said to help remove excess twist! Stitching with doubled thread will give traditional sashiko, especially *moyōzashi*, the 'big stitch'

look, and extra warmth. It also means there is no loose end to become frayed and worn. Tie the ends in a single knot.

Starting and finishing with a knot

Begin by holding the two ends together and tying an ordinary single knot (sometimes called a quilter's knot). The needle can't escape – useful if you are working on the floor in dim light, as in old farmhouses where a lost needle could be trodden on. Begin stitching with the single knot on the back of your work. The knots don't show on the front. *Hitomezashi* always begins and ends this way, or else it could unravel. If you are using wadding (batting) and want a neat back, it is possible with fine thread to 'pop the knot' by pulling it through the backing fabric into the wadding, or through the top fabric if it is a looser weave, and begin as if hand quilting. When you get to the end, take

the needle to the back and wrap the thread around it once. Hold this point between thumb and forefinger, so the knot can't travel further up the thread, and pull the needle through. If you have left yourself with too little thread to do this, remember you only need about 2.5cm (1in) of thread to tie the knot with the eye end of the needle. See overleaf for using a *hatamusubi* (loom knot) to join on new threads.

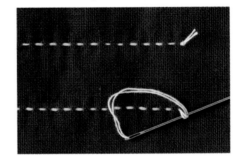

above: Starting and finishing with a knot (shown from the back of the stitching).

Can sashiko be stitched by machine?

Some sashiko patterns make lovely machine quilting designs, especially continuous line patterns such as *shippō tsunagi* (page 64), *sayagata* (page 90) or *kasumi tsunagi* (page 71). However, the finished effect

is quite different. Machine quilting makes a hard, continuous line and the effect of the little running stitches is lost. Even with the imitation hand quilting stitch on many modern high-tech machines, it still doesn't look the

same. The machine lockstitch is akin to couching rather than hand running stitch, which defeats the traditional purpose of sashiko. Machine quilted Japanese patterns are fun to do, but you can't really call it sashiko!

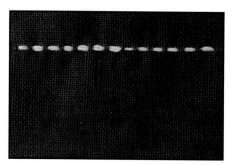

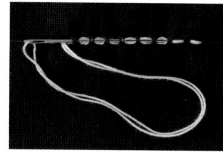

Starting and finishing without a knot

This is possible for *moyōzashi* designs and is preferable for items seen from both sides, but a knot is still the more secure option. You could try this knotless method if stitching sashiko on a quilt, to keep the back neat. Start by taking several stitches towards the start of the stitch line, going in the opposite direction to your planned route, then turn around and stitch back over your first stitches, sewing back through the original thread. At the end of the thread, repeat this in reverse – about ½–1in (1.3–2.5cm) of overlapped stitches will be enough to stop stitches coming undone. This method was used on the old *furoshiki* (wrapping cloth) on page 14 and also on the bamboo and snow-flake *kamon* (family crest) on page 93.

Stitch size

Moyōzashi stitches on old items vary greatly in size, from tiny stitches on a *furoshiki* (page 14) to enormous ones on a *kotatsu* table cover (page 37 behind cushions). It seems to depend on the number of layers being stitched – more layers mean bigger stitches. Between four and eight stitches to 1in (2.5cm) is about right. Evenness is more important than stitch size.

In *moyōzashi*, the gap between the stitches is about half the length of the stitch. Count stitches in short sections of the pattern or use inter-secting pattern lines to help gauge your stitches. Like hand quilting, you will find your sashiko settles down to a regular stitch length with practise. *Hitomezashi* stitches relate to the grid size (see page 96).

Making a hatamusubi (loom knot)

In Japan in the past, sashiko thread was precious so a *hatamusubi* (loom knot) was used to get the most out of even the last half inch. The harder this joining knot is pulled, the tighter it becomes. To make tying the knot easier, moisten the ends of the doubled thread so they stick together (shown as one thread in the diagrams below. The method is the same for right and left-handed people – both hands do equal amounts of work! The secret is in the way the short ends of thread are held whilst the knot is tied. Practise using different coloured threads.

1 Leave 1in (2.5cm) tail of old thread loose on the back of work (shown in white). Thread the needle but don't knot new thread. Lay the end(s) of the new thread (in red) against the back of the work.

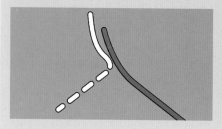

2 Hold the end of the new thread between the first two fingers of your left hand (at point A). Use your left thumb to bend the tail of the old thread over the new. Put your thumb on the crossed threads to hold them. Keep holding these two points until instructed otherwise.

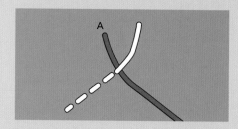

3 Now the long part of the new thread does most of the work. Loop it to the left, as shown by the arrow. Lift your thumb quickly, pass the thread under it and hold the crossed threads again.

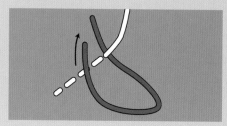

4 Take the long part of the new thread under its own tail and over the old thread, so the new thread makes a loop.

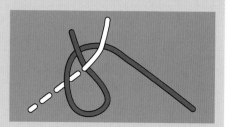

5 Continue to hold the thread at point A. Use your left thumb to bend the old thread through the loop and hold the end between left thumb and left ring finger at point B. Holding the two short ends so they can't flip out of the knot, use the long new thread to gently pull the knot closed with your right hand.

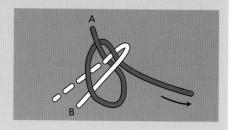

Sewing sashiko

In Japanese sewing, the needle is held still and the fabric placed on it in a pleating action, several stitches at a time, rather than making individual stitches with the needle being moved through fixed fabric. A quilting frame is therefore not used and sashiko is not stitched from the centre outwards, like Western quilting, but from side to side.

Begin stitching at one side of the pattern and work across. Traditionally, a *kakehari* (see page 16) is used to hold large pieces of fabric under tension. Push the needle through when it is full and smooth the stitches out between thumb and forefinger, but don't fluff up the thread by scraping it with your nails. The double thread lies parallel in the stitch and patterns appear quite bold with a textured effect. Taking one stitch at a time will twist the threads and spoil your sashiko. You can use a coin thimble (see page 16) to help push the needle through or just hold the needle as you would normally.

Sashiko stitching – right and wrong

Watch out for the following points, particularly when stitching *moyōzashi* designs.

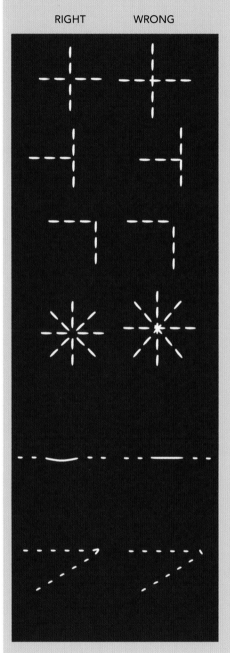

RIGHT   WRONG

Where pattern lines meet, space the stitches so they don't touch – this will make the pattern look more elegant.

When turning corners, make the last stitch right into the corner so the pattern will be sharply defined.

Where pattern lines cross, make a slightly longer gap between stitches, so stitches don't cross on the right side, making an ugly lump (and a weak point). Avoid joining in new threads at these points. Remember, in some *hitomezashi* patterns the stitches are supposed to cross.

Where indicated in some patterns, strand loosely across the back of your work. For a quilt where the back will be seen, run the thread between the backing and wadding (batting).

When you make a sharp change of direction, leave a little loop on the back for ease, especially when stitching *hitomezashi* patterns, or your sashiko will pucker up!

Ready for the projects?

So, are you ready to get started? I hope so, because the projects that follow have been specially designed to make your sashiko look wonderful and to allow you to create beautiful things from even the smallest practice sample. You can make the projects exactly as shown in the photographs or you can easily replace the patterns with your own favourites from the Pattern Library (pages 58–109). Like the project section, the Pattern Library starts with easier designs, working through to the most challenging sashiko patterns, with an extra section for motifs. There are an incredible 70 different *moyōzashi* patterns and 50 *hitomezashi* designs and variations in the library. If you work through the patterns, trying to resist the temptation to go for the hardest first, you will soon become a sashiko expert!

LONG SAMPLERS

Small samples are a good way to practise new sashiko patterns and need not be forgotten in your work basket afterwards. Ready-made picture frames make a feature of your stitching for a lovely gift. I used simple unvarnished frames and three different shades of indigo fabric for these samples. The narrow frames, just 10 x 4in (25.4 x 10.2cm), meant I could use up fabric oddments. The patterns are (from left to right): *asanoha* (hemp leaf), *fundō* (scale weights) and *jūji kikkō* (cross tortoiseshell).

> **Sashiko patterns used**
> *asanoha* page 72; *fundō* page 65 and *jūji kikkō* page 86
> **Finished size of samplers shown** 10 x 4in (25.4 x 10.2cm)

You will need

- Small frame of your choice
- Piece of self-adhesive mounting card, same size as frame backing board
- Piece of sashiko fabric at least ½in (1.3cm) larger than frame size all round
- Fine sashiko thread
- Basic sewing and marking kit (page 16)

> **Tip**
>
> Commercial frame sizes normally refer to the size of the backing board or image rather than the measurement outside the moulding, eg a 6 x 4in (15.2 x 10.2cm) frame will fit a picture that size. Remember, the visible image area will be up to ¼in (6mm) smaller all round.

1 Marking and stitching the sashiko: Remove any glass in the frame and store carefully. Use the inside of the frame aperture to mark the working area on your fabric. Select a design from the Pattern Library, mark it on the fabric (see page 22) and then stitch your sashiko design (see page 25).

2 Framing the samplers: Lightly press your finished sashiko from the back. Arrange the sashiko on the self-adhesive mounting card, make sure the fabric grain is straight and then press the sampler into place.

3 Replace the glass in the frame and put the sashiko panel behind it. Replace any necessary packing in the back of the frame and fasten the grips in place.

GREETINGS CARDS

New Year celebrations in Japan rival Christmas in Europe and the USA but whatever the festive occasion a handmade greetings card is always extra special. These pretty cards use 4in (10.2cm) square samples of sashiko for a bold graphic effect – from left to right, *komezashi* (rice stitch) in coloured threads, a single *asanoha* (hemp leaf) and *ganzezashi* (sea urchin). The designs could be framed instead (see the long samplers on page 26). The decorative hook rack I've used is really a fancy photo frame. It holds a lucky New Year arrow and an antique *kasuri* ikat *haori* (formal jacket) and has *hitomezashi* inserts – *kawari kikkōzashi* (tortoiseshell variation), *ajirozashi* (threaded stitch) and *jijūhishikaha* (woven cross diamond). I used coloured and variegated threads to add interest.

Sashiko patterns used
Komezashi page 97, single *asanoha* page 72 and *ganzezashi* page 66
Finished size of card 5in (12.7cm) square with 3in (7.6cm) aperture

You will need

- Card blank, photograph frame or other item with aperture to fit your embroidery
- Piece of sashiko fabric at least ½in (1.3cm) larger than aperture size all round
- Lightweight iron-on interfacing, same size as sashiko fabric
- Fine or medium sashiko thread (exact quantity depends on sashiko pattern selected)
- Masking tape or double-sided adhesive tape
- Basic sewing and marking kit (see page 16)

1 **Marking and stitching the sashiko:** Use the inside of the card aperture or photograph frame as a stencil to mark the working area on your fabric. Select a design from the Pattern Library and mark the fabric (see marking methods, page 22). Stitch your sashiko design (see page 25).

2 Lightly press your finished sashiko from the back. Following the manufacturer's instructions, iron the interfacing on to the back of the sashiko. Trim raw edges back to the interfacing if necessary.

3 **Mounting the sashiko into a card:** Open out the card blank, arrange the sashiko behind the card aperture and use masking tape to hold it in place. If you are using a double-fold card blank as shown in **Fig 1** below, the extra fold will hide the back of the sashiko. If your card has a single fold, shown in **Fig 2**, use a piece of paper and double-sided tape to cover the back of the sashiko neatly.

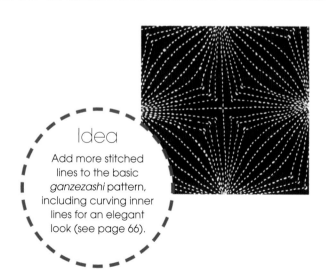

Idea

Add more stitched lines to the basic *ganzezashi* pattern, including curving inner lines for an elegant look (see page 66).

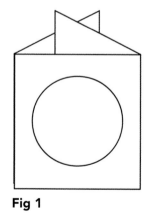

Fig 1

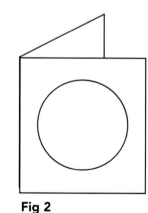

Fig 2

4 **Mounting the sashiko into a frame:** Position the sashiko panel behind the glass in the frame, replace any packing in the back of the frame and fasten the frame grips in place.

COASTER COLLECTION

Single sashiko motifs such as *sakura* (cherry blossom), *ume* (plum) and *kikyō* (Chinese bellflower) look very pretty stitched in variegated threads and made into simple coasters. You can also stitch single repeats of larger sashiko patterns like *hiragumi manji tsunagi* (linked manji). *Hitomezashi* (one stitch sashiko) practice pieces are also ideal for small items as this coaster collection shows. Use oddments of coloured threads to make corner tassels (described below).

Sashiko patterns used (below, left to right)
Kakinohanazashi and variation page 100, *hiragumi manji tsunagi* page 81, *nagarebishi* page 106, five floral motifs page 92, *komezashi* variation page 97, *hanabishizashi* page 105 and *honzenizashi* (see *zenizashi* page 99)
Finished size of coaster 3½in (8.9cm) square

For one coaster you will need

- Sashiko fabric 4in (10.2cm) square
- Square of butter muslin, slightly larger than sashiko squares (optional)
- Patchwork cotton 4in (10.2cm) square, for backing
- Fine or medium sashiko thread (exact quantity depends on sashiko pattern selected)
- Variegated perlé thread (optional)
- Sewing thread to tone with fabric
- Basic sewing and marking kit (see page 16)
- Sewing machine

1 **Marking and stitching the sashiko:** If you wish to use a muslin layer, tack (baste) a piece of muslin to the back the sashiko fabric (see page 22) and stitch the sashiko pattern through both layers (see page 25). Press lightly when all stitching is complete.

2 **Making up a coaster:** Place a square of backing fabric right sides together with a sashiko sample, pin and machine sew around the square with a ¼in (6mm) seam allowance, leaving 2½in (6.4cm) unsewn on one side. Snip the points off the corners, but do not cut right up to the stitches – leave about ⅛in (3mm). Turn the coaster right side out and push the corners out. Turn in the raw edges of the gap and slipstitch together invisibly. Press lightly.

3 Use scraps of thread to make simple corner 'tassels' by threading two strands through each corner, tying in a knot and trimming to about 1in (2.5cm) long. See also page 55.

Idea
Why not turn the coaster into a pincushion for your sashiko needles by stuffing it with wadding (batting) scraps?

Idea
Use two larger fabric pieces, about 10in (25.4cm) square, to make a traditional *fukin* (cloth) to use as a mat. Sew together following step 2, before sewing the sashiko through two layers. Old *fukin* are usually squarish rectangles with very basic sashiko (see page 10). Originally used as dusters and cleaning cloths, the prettiest are called *hana* (flower) *fukin*.

MOMOYAMA TABLE MATS

These elegant table mats feature two similar sashiko patterns, just right for a special dinner for two. The design is divided with a diagonal zigzag called *matsukawabishi* (pine bark diamond), a style of dividing patterns introduced in Japan in the Momoyama era (1568–1615). I used *hishi seigaiha* (diamond blue waves) for the blue mat and *hishi manji* (diamond *manji*) for the ochre one. The colours alternate between the two, so the blue mat has an autumnal ochre *momiji* (see maple leaf in Motifs, page 92) and the ochre mat has a late summer blue *kikyō* (see bellflower in Motifs, page 92). The backing fabrics, showing slightly at the sides, contrast with the main colour – a feature copied from kimono hems. The sashiko is stitched through two layers (optional).

> **Sashiko patterns used**
> Blue mat – *hishi seigaiha* page 83 and *momiji* page 92
> Ochre mat – *hishi manji* page 83 and *kikyō* page 92
> **Finished size of mat** 12 x 14in (30.5 x 35.5cm)

For each mat you will need

- Sashiko fabric 13 x 15in (33 x 38cm)
- Backing fabric 13 x 15½in (33 x 39.4cm)
- Butter muslin, slightly larger than sashiko fabric (optional)
- Sashiko thread in medium cream (exact quantity depends on sashiko pattern selected)
- Medium coloured or variegated sashiko thread
- Sewing thread to tone with fabric
- Basic sewing and marking kit (see page 16)
- Sewing machine

1 Marking and stitching the sashiko:
Zigzag the edges of the sashiko fabrics
to prevent fraying. Select a sashiko
pattern based on a diagonal grid from
the Pattern Library. On the sashiko
fabric, mark a 1 x ½in (2.5 x 1.3cm)
diagonal grid in an area 14 x 12in
(35.6 x 30.5cm), leaving a ½in (1.3cm)
seam allowance all round (see marking
methods, page 22). The large diamonds
in both *hishi seigaiha* and *hishi manji*
are 4 x 2in (10.2 x 5.1cm) – see **Fig 1** for
basic layout. If you are using a muslin
layer, tack (baste) a piece of muslin to
the back of each piece of sashiko fabric
and stitch the sashiko through both
layers (see tacking fabric layers, page
22). Stitch the diamond pattern in
cream thread (for both mats). Mark and
stitch the leaf or flower detail, then
stitch the background with diagonal
lines. Lightly press finished the sashiko
from the wrong side.

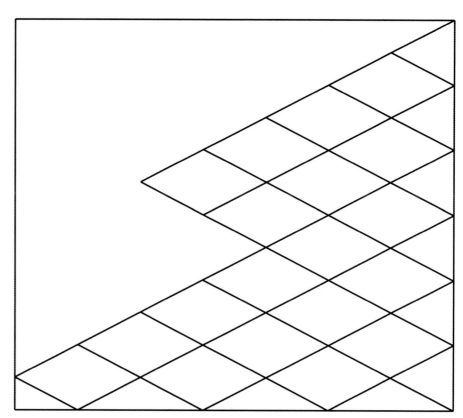

Fig 1

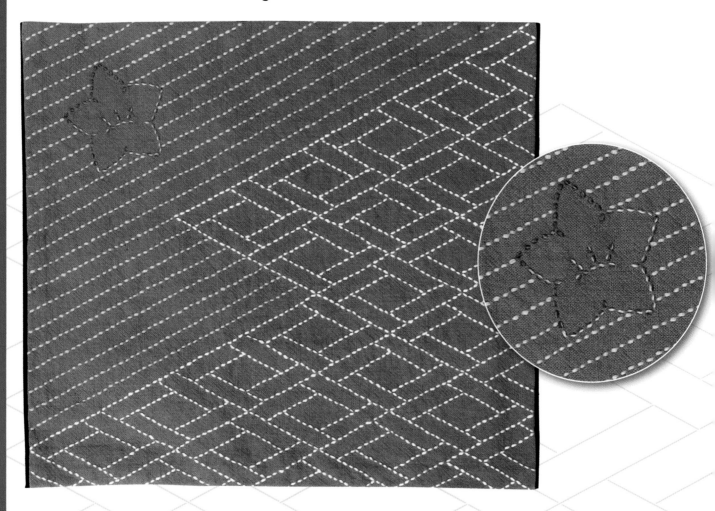

Idea

Falling maple leaves are an autumnal image but you could easily make mats for other seasons. Change the leaves to *sakura* (cherry blossoms) for spring or make a New Year set with *shō chiku bai* (pine, plum and bamboo). See Motifs within the Pattern Library (page 92) for more ideas and designs.

❷ **Making up a table mat:** Place one front panel and a contrasting backing piece right sides together, and pin the ends only, lining up the cut edges (see **Fig 2**). Note: the back panel will be longer than the front, so approximately ⅛in (3mm) will show at either end of the finished mat, echoing the thread colour. Sew the panel and backing together at the ends only, using ½in (1.3cm) seams. Press the seams towards the front panel as indicated in Fig 2.

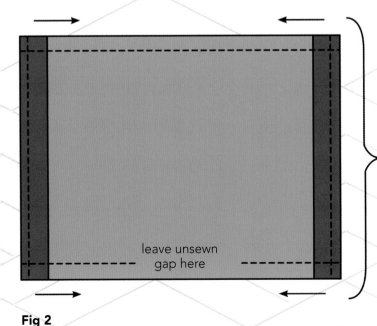

press side seams towards sashiko panel

leave unsewn gap here

Fig 2

❸ Pin the top and bottom edges and machine sew together, leaving a 4in (10.2cm) gap in the centre of the lower edge. Trim off the corners within the seam allowance but do not cut right up to the stitches – about halfway is fine. Bag out the panel, i.e., turn it the right way out through the unsewn gap. Ease the corners out so they are nice and sharp. Lay the mat flat and smooth it out. The backing fabric will show as a narrow strip at the ends – hold it in place with small, neat hand stitches through backing and seam allowances only. Turn under the raw edges at the bottom of the mat, pin or tack (baste) and then slipstitch the gap closed. Make the other mat in the same way.

SAMPLER CUSHIONS

Some sashiko patterns fit together very well for more elaborate arrangements as these striking cushions show. Choose patterns that share the same base grid and they will fit together with ease. The blue cushion is patterned with five different hexagon and diamond designs on a ¾ x ⅜in (1.9 x 1cm) grid. The beige cushion (also shown on page 39) has variations on the basic *kakinohanazashi* (persimmon flower stitch) with an Ainu embroidery design (see page 13) in chain stitch on the side borders. The late winter landscape of northern Japan provided the colour inspiration for the variegated threads while raw silk gives a touch of luxury to the blue cushion and the beige cushion's border. The sashiko has been stitched through two layers, with muslin stabilizing the silk.

Sashiko patterns used
Blue cushion (top to bottom) – *hishi moyō* page 82,
kasane kikkō page 88, *jūji kikkō* page 86,
arare kikkō page 87 and *yosegi* page 89
Beige cushion – *kakinohanazashi* and variations page 100
Finished cushion size 18in (45.7cm) square

You will need

For each cushion
Sewing thread to tone with fabrics

Basic sewing and marking kit (see page 16)

Two pieces of toning silk dupion 19 x 12in
(48.3 x 30.5cm), for the cushion back

Cushion pad 18in (45.7cm) square

Sewing machine

(See overleaf for individual cushion requirements)

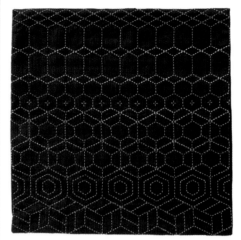

BLUE CUSHION

❶ Marking and stitching the sashiko:
Tack (baste) the piece of muslin to the back of the raw silk and zigzag the edges to prevent fraying (see tacking fabric layers, page 22). Mark and stitch the sashiko by first marking a ¾ x ⅜in (1.9 x 1cm) diagonal grid in an 18in (45.7cm) square area on the raw silk, leaving a ½in (1.3cm) seam allowance all round (see marking methods, page 22). The pattern layout for the blue cushion is shown in **Fig 1** below. Stitch sashiko through both layers and, when finished, lightly press the sashiko from the wrong side.

❷ Making up the cushion: Assemble the cushion, using ½in (1.3cm) seams throughout. Turn a ¼in (6mm) hem along one of the long sides on each piece of backing fabric. Zigzag the remaining raw edges. Place the sashiko and one backing piece right sides together and pin, as shown in **Fig 2a**. Pin the second backing piece right sides together and overlapping the first piece (**Fig 2b**). Machine sew around the edges, with ½in (1.3cm) seam allowance, leaving a gap for turning. Clip the corners, turn right side out and insert the cushion pad through the gap to finish.

You will need

- Blue raw silk 19in (48.3cm) square
- Piece of butter muslin, slightly larger than the silk
- Medium variegated sashiko thread (the exact quantity depends on the sashiko patterns selected)

Fig 1 Blue cushion patterns

All these patterns were drawn on a ¾ x ⅜in (1.9 x 1cm) diagonal grid. From top to bottom: *hishi moyō* (diamond pattern), *kasane kikkō* (layered tortoiseshell diamonds), *jūji kikkō* ('10' cross tortoiseshell), *arare kikkō* (hailstone or segmented tortoiseshell) and *yosegi* (mosaic or parquetry blocks).

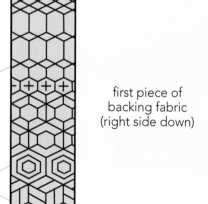

first piece of backing fabric (right side down)

Fig 2a

both pieces of backing fabric overlapping and sewn in place

Fig 2b

Tip

If you prefer a zip opening in your cushions, see the floor cushions on page 54 for instructions.

BEIGE CUSHION

❶ Marking and stitching the sashiko:
Machine sew the piece of raw silk to either side of the sashiko fabric with a ½in (1.3cm) seam allowance. Press the seam towards the silk. Tack (baste) the piece of muslin to the back of the raw silk and zigzag the edges, to prevent fraying (see tacking fabric layers, page 22). Mark and stitch the sashiko (see **Fig 1** below for the border pattern). On the sashiko fabric, mark a ³⁄₈in (1cm) grid all over and then stitch the sashiko pattern through both layers – see page 100 for *kakinohanazashi* and related variations. Lightly press the finished sashiko from the wrong side.

❷ Making up the cushion: Assemble and make up the beige cushion in the same way as described for the blue cushion in step 2 opposite.

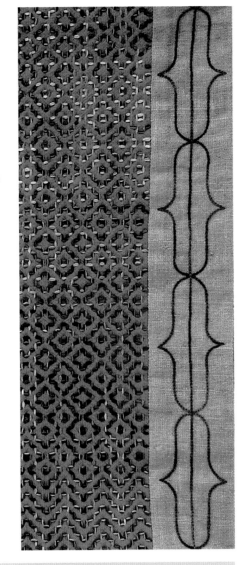

Idea

Variations on *komezashi* (pages 97 and 98) also combine well for a sampler and are effective worked with variegated threads.

You will need

- Sashiko fabric of your choice 19 x 14in (48.3 x 35.6cm)
- Two pieces of beige raw silk 19in x 3in (48.3 x 7.6cm), for the borders
- Piece of butter muslin, slightly larger than the completed front panel
- Fine variegated perlé cotton, for border embroidery

Fig 1 Beige cushion border

I adapted the border design for the beige cushion from an antique apron, one of several old sashiko pieces I have seen with Ainu designs from Hokkaido. I worked it in chain stitch (see Fig 2, right), as in the original. The Ainu call it *ayus* (having a thorn). It is an elongated version of *amimon* (fishing nets, page 70), with an extra vertical line, and is drawn in the same way. Each repeat shape is 4in (10.2cm) long and the curves were drawn with a 1in (2.5cm) circle template.

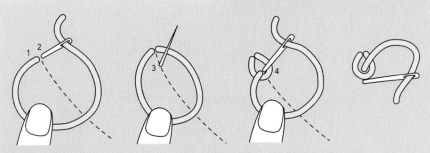

Fig 2
To work chain stitch, bring the needle out at 1 and down at 2, creating a loop. Bring the needle up at 3, inside the loop and pull the loop to form a chain. Put the needle down at 4 to create the next loop and continue this way until the end. To finish, anchor the last loop with a small stitch.

SASHIKO TOTE BAGS

The front of a tote bag is a good place to show off a sashiko panel, especially when it is as bright as this one. Some old sashiko pieces use a woven check or stripe to line up the stitches, so I experimented with a woven check, using the pattern lines rather than marking a grid before stitching a *komezashi* (rice stitch) variation. It is an old stitch used on fishermen's *donza* coats but the bright fabric, denim border and orange lining gives it a contemporary look. The idea is taken a step further with the bag shown on page 43, made from checked fabric, with *shippō tsunagi* (linked seven treasures) and *hirai jūmon* (crossed well curb) stitched in gorgeous rainbow sashiko thread.

Sashiko patterns used
Denim tote bag – *komezashi* variation page 97
Checked tote bag – *shippō tsunagi* page 64
and *hirai jūmon* page 79
Finished size of denim bag 12 x 16in (30.5 x 40.6cm)
Finished size of checked bag 19¼ x 13¾in (48.9 x 34.9cm)

For the denim bag you will need

- Checked fabric 12 x 9in (30.5 x 22.8cm)
- Butter muslin, slightly larger than checked fabric (optional)
- Medium weight denim:
  two pieces 3½ x 9in (8.9 x 22.8cm), for top and bottom borders
  two pieces 3 x 17in (7.6 x 43.2cm), for side borders
  one piece 13 x 17in (33 x 43.2cm), for back
- Medium sashiko thread (exact quantity depends on sashiko pattern selected)
- Two pieces of orange cotton fabric 13 x 17in (33 x 43.2cm), for lining
- Two 12in (30.5cm) lengths of 1in (2.5cm) wide cotton webbing for straps
- Basic sewing and marking kit (see page 16)
- Sewing machine

Tip
Choose a suitable size for the pattern. A ¾in (1.9cm) check is perfect for this *komezashi* variation.

DENIM TOTE BAG

1 Marking and stitching the sashiko: If you are using the optional muslin layer, tack (baste) a piece of muslin to the back of the checked fabric and stitch sashiko through both layers (see tacking fabric layers, page 22). Zigzag the edges of the sashiko fabrics to prevent fraying. Select and stitch the sashiko pattern of your choice – *hitomezashi* patterns (pages 96–109) work best on a small grid. Lightly press the finished sashiko from the wrong side.

2 Assembling the front panel: With right sides together, machine sew one 9 x 3½in (22.8 x 8.9cm) piece of denim to the top of the centre panel, using a ½in (1.3cm) seam. Sew the second 9 x 3½in (22.8 x 8.9cm) piece to the bottom and press both seams outwards. Machine sew the 17 x 3in (43.2 x 7.6cm) pieces to either side of the front panel, using ½in (1.3cm) seams. Press seams outwards.

Making Fabric Straps

If you can't buy webbing, you can make simple straps from the same fabric used for the bag.

1 Cut two pieces of fabric 12 x 3in (30.5cm x 7.6cm), along the grain i.e. parallel to the selvedge, so they won't stretch when you use the bag. Turn under and press ¼in (6mm) along both long sides as shown in the diagram.

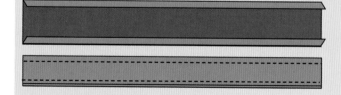

2 Fold the first strap in half lengthwise and machine sew along the strip, about ⅛in (3mm) from each edge. Repeat for the second strap.

40

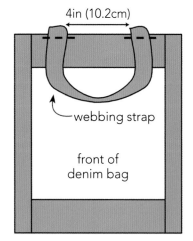

4in (10.2cm)

webbing strap

front of
denim bag

Fig 1a

4in (10.2cm)

webbing strap

back of
denim bag

Fig 1b

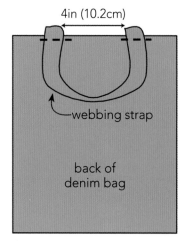

3 **Making up the bag:** Arrange the webbing straps on the right side of the bag front and back panels as shown in **Figs 1a** and **1b**, allowing the strap ends to overlap the edge of the bag panel by ½in (1.3cm). The gap between the straps ends is 4in (10.2cm). Make sure the straps are the same length and not twisted. Tack (baste) in place.

4 With the bag front and back panels right sides together and using a ¼in (6mm) seam, machine sew down the side, across the bottom and up the other side – shown by the dashed line in **Fig 2**. Clip the corners within the seam allowance but don't cut right up to the stitches – leave about ⅛in (3mm). Press the seam to one side to complete the bag outer section.

outer bag

Fig 2

leave gap

bag lining

Fig 3

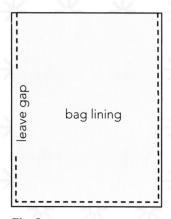

5 Make the lining by placing the two pieces of orange cotton fabric right sides together and, with a ¼in (6mm) seam, machine sew down the side, across the bottom and up part of the other side, as shown in **Fig 3**. Leave a 4in (10.2cm) gap unsewn and sew the remaining side seam. The bag will be turned right side out through the unsewn gap. Press the seam to one side.

6 Turn the outer bag section right side out. Keeping the bag lining turned inside out, place the bag outer inside the lining, lining up the top edge and side seams. Make sure the side seams are lined up so they are pressed in alternate directions, i.e., the bag outer side seam allowances should lie in the opposite direction to the lining seam allowances to avoid a lump where the seams line up, as shown in **Fig 4**. Machine sew around the top of the bag, sewing the lining to the bag outer all round with a ¼in (6mm) seam.

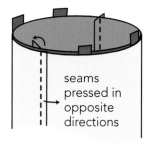

seams pressed in opposite directions

Fig 4

7 Turn the bag right side out through the unsewn gap in the lining side seam. Press the seam at the top of the bag. Machine or hand sew around the top of the bag, about ⅛in (3mm) from the edge. Turn the bag inside out and slipstitch the gap in the lining closed to finish.

CHECKED TOTE BAG

1 **Marking and stitching the sashiko:** If you are using the optional muslin layer, tack (baste) a piece of muslin to the back of the checked fabric (see tacking fabric layers, page 22). Zigzag the edges of the fabrics to prevent fraying. Select the sashiko pattern of your choice: *hirai jūmon* (crossed well curb) has plain squares as part of the pattern but *shippō tsunagi* (linked seven treasures) was modified by only stitching on the white and dark blue squares. Stitch sashiko through both layers and, when finished, press lightly from the wrong side.

2 **Making up the bag:** Follow steps 3–7 of the denim bag opposite on page 42 for making up the checked bag and its lining.

One side of the checked bag uses the *shippō tsunagi* pattern (above), with *hirai jūmon* on the other side (right).

Tip
Use the size of very large check patterns to determine the size of your bag – say five checks by seven – and keep the squares whole. The check on my fabric measures 2¾in (7cm), so my finished bag is 19¼ x 13¾in (48.9 x 34.9cm). Remember to add a seam allowance all round and cut the lining the same size. These sashiko patterns would also work well on a patchwork of squares.

Idea
Hirasan kuzushi (simple three lines form, page 76) has plain squares as part of the pattern and many larger sashiko patterns are based on a grid that work at this scale. My idea for working on a large check came from an old *sodenashi* waistcoat from Sakata city which had a different pattern in every square. Vintage sashiko on such a large check pattern is quite rare. You could use the idea to make a sampler bag.

Idea
For a more traditional look, try a *kamon* (family crest, page 93). Crests were often stitched on *furoshiki* (wrapping cloths). The paulownia crest featured on this bag (left) was used by the Tokugawa shoguns.

For the checked bag you will need

- Two pieces of checked fabric 20¼ x 14¾in (51.4 x 37.5cm) (see Tip top right)
- Two pieces of butter muslin, slightly larger than checked fabric (optional)
- Medium rainbow sashiko thread (exact quantity depends on pattern selected)
- Two pieces of cotton fabric 20¼ x 14¾in (51.4 x 37.5cm), for lining
- Two 12in (30.5cm) lengths of 1in (2.5cm) wide cotton webbing, for straps
- Basic sewing and marking kit (see page 16)

NOREN CURTAIN

Noren are special curtains hung over open doors in Japan. They are the modern version of the fabric screens used to partition the large halls of Heian era (794–1185) aristocratic residences. Today they are also used by shops and restaurants to show that they are open. *Noren* are useful at home to screen open doorways in summer or just to hide a messy sewing room from view! Simple piecing makes the background like a mountain, with individual appliqué *matsukawabishi* (pine bark diamond) shapes filled in with various patterns – the same shapes that link to make the tessellated *matsukawabishi* sashiko pattern on page 84. The appliqué patches are a reference to old, patched work clothes but the sashiko could be stitched on plain cloth.

Sashiko patterns used
Right panel (from top) – *hishi moyō* page 82, *higaki* page 77 and *kawari sayagata* page 91
Left panel (from top) – *nanamehōgan tsunagi* page 75 and *kagome* page 83
Finished size of curtain 37½ x 30in (95.3 x 76.2cm)

Fig 1

You will need

- Plain blue fabric 40 x 16¾in (102 x 42.5cm)
- Plain rust fabric 40 x 16¾in (102 x 42.5cm)
- Five pieces of patterned fabric 8 x 10in (20.3 x 25.4cm), for appliqué
- Five pieces of plain blue fabric 10 x 4in (25.4 x 10.2cm), for tabs
- Plain rust fabric 8 x 2in (20.3 x 5.1cm), for decorative knot
- Two pieces of butter muslin 40 x 17in (102 x 43.2cm)
- Two pieces of plain fabric 39 x 16in (100 x 40.6cm), for backing
- Fine sashiko thread (the exact quantity depends on the sashiko pattern selected)
- Sewing thread to tone with fabrics
- Basic sewing and marking kit (see page 16)
- Sewing machine

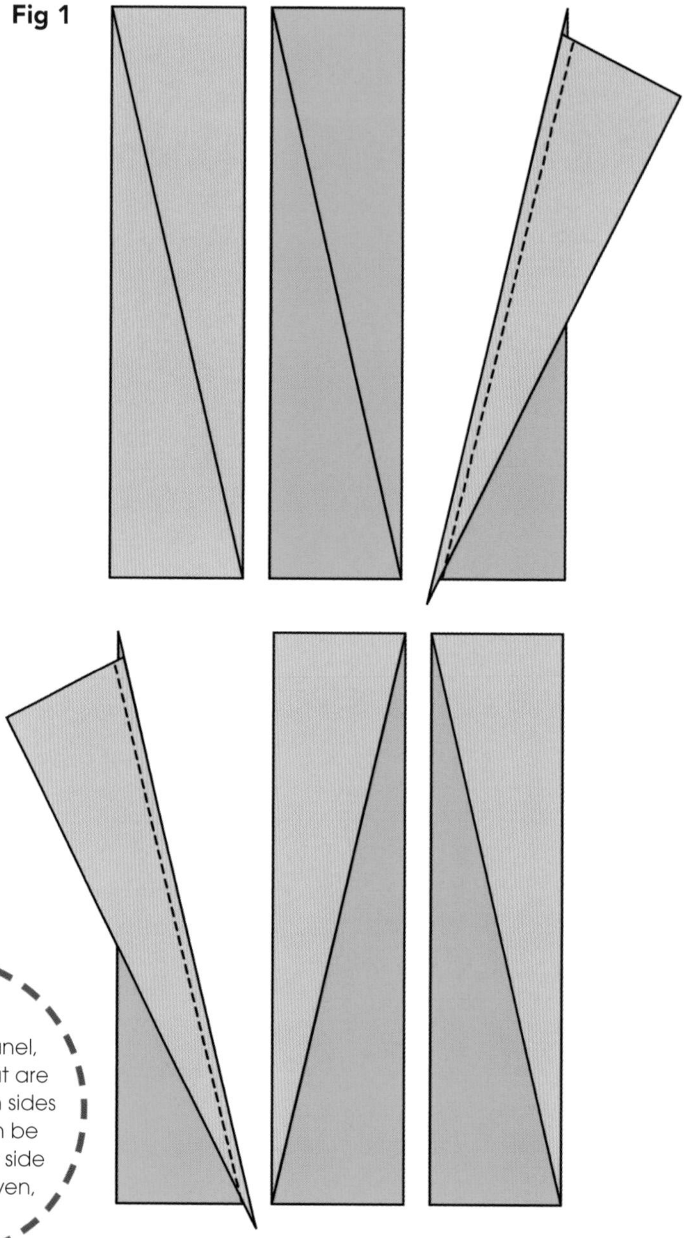

1 Making the mountain panel: With reference to **Fig 1**, draw a diagonal line from corner to corner on each 40 x 16¾in (102 x 42.5cm) piece of plain blue and plain rust fabric and cut to make two triangles in each colour. Flip one piece of each over (using the back as the right side) and pin together. Machine sew one blue triangle to one rust triangle with a ¼in (6mm) seam allowance, taking care not to stretch the bias edge. Press seams towards the blue.

Tip
For the main panel, select fabrics that are the same on both sides so the back can be used as the right side i.e., plain or woven, not prints.

44

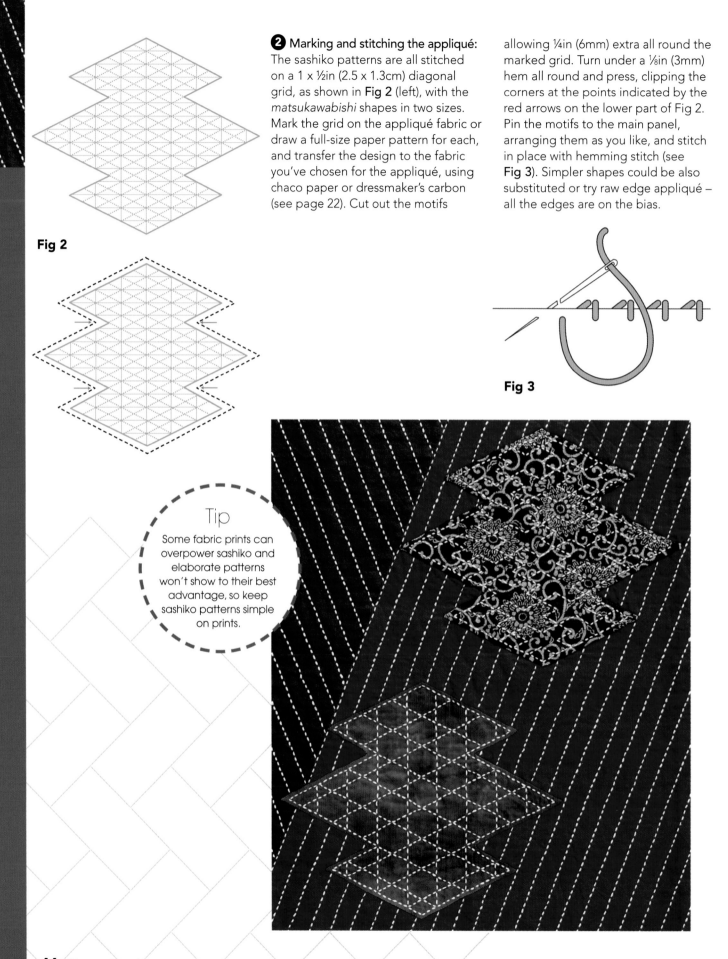

2 **Marking and stitching the appliqué:** The sashiko patterns are all stitched on a 1 x ½in (2.5 x 1.3cm) diagonal grid, as shown in **Fig 2** (left), with the *matsukawabishi* shapes in two sizes. Mark the grid on the appliqué fabric or draw a full-size paper pattern for each, and transfer the design to the fabric you've chosen for the appliqué, using chaco paper or dressmaker's carbon (see page 22). Cut out the motifs allowing ¼in (6mm) extra all round the marked grid. Turn under a ⅛in (3mm) hem all round and press, clipping the corners at the points indicated by the red arrows on the lower part of Fig 2. Pin the motifs to the main panel, arranging them as you like, and stitch in place with hemming stitch (see **Fig 3**). Simpler shapes could be also substituted or try raw edge appliqué – all the edges are on the bias.

Fig 2

Fig 3

Tip

Some fabric prints can overpower sashiko and elaborate patterns won't show to their best advantage, so keep sashiko patterns simple on prints.

❸ Tack (baste) a piece of muslin to the back of the each panel (see tacking fabric layers, page 22). Mark and stitch the sashiko, working the *matsukawabishi* outline shapes first. Stitch the diagonal parallel lines in the background ½in (1.3cm) apart.

❹ **Making up the curtain:** Place each front panel and backing fabric right sides together and pin all round. Machine sew with a ½in (1.3cm) seam allowance, leaving an 8in (20.3cm) gap at the centre of the lower edge. Trim off the corners within the seam allowance but do not cut right up to the stitches – leave about ⅛in (3mm). Bag out the panel, i.e., turn it the right way out through the unsewn gap. Ease the corners out so they are nice and sharp. Lay the panel flat and smooth it out. Turn under the raw edges at the bottom of the panel, pin or tack (baste) and slipstitch the gap closed. From the back, sew right

around the panel ¼in (6mm) from the edge with small, neat hand stitches through backing and seam allowances only, to keep the backing in place. Place the two panels side by side. With sashiko thread, hand sew the panels together with Cretan stitch (see **Fig 4**) from the top down, for about 5in (12.7cm).

❺ Make tabs for the curtain using the five 10 x 4in (25.4 x 10.2cm) pieces of plain blue fabric and following the instructions for making fabric bag straps on page 40. Turn the raw ends under and hand sew the tabs to the top of the curtain, positioning them as shown in the picture above. Finish the tabs by stab stitching through all layers, following the pattern in **Fig 5**. Make another strip using the 8 x 2in (20.3 x 5.1cm) piece of plain rust fabric. Loosely tie this strip into a single knot (shown below) and then stitch it to the top of the curtain opening for a traditional good luck charm.

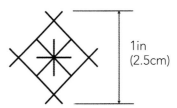

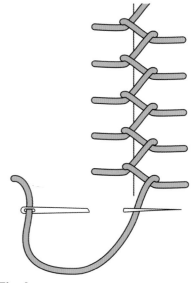

Fig 4

Cretan stitch is a variation on blanket stitch, with alternate stitches in opposite directions, giving a plaited effect. To join two panels, place them side by side and take a stitch through each panel alternately, stabbing through all layers. Start and finish with a knot on the wrong side.

1in (2.5cm)

Fig 5

KINCHAKU BAGS

These pretty drawstring bags are called *kinchaku*, a word derived from *kin* (width) and *chaku* (to wear). In Japan, they are used as kimono accessories and are popular items for decorating with sashiko. They would also make handy workbags for all your sashiko bits and pieces. Try stitching a different sashiko pattern on the front and back. I used *nowaki* ('grasses') and *seigaiha* (blue ocean waves) on the blue bag and *matsukawabishi* (pine bark diamond), *kagome* (woven bamboo) and *komezashi* (rice stitch) on the red. As the bags are small, I worked the sashiko without wadding (batting) or backing.

Sashiko patterns used
Nowaki page 69; *seigaiha* variation page 69; *matsukawabishi* page 84; *kagome* page 83 and *komezashi* page 97
Finished bag size 10½ x 8in (26.7 x 20.3cm)

You will need

For each bag
Fine sashiko thread
Variegated perlé thread No 8
Two 25in (63.5cm) lengths of cord for drawstring
Two pieces of plain cotton 3½in (8.9cm) square for flower trims
Basic sewing and marking kit (page 16)

For the blue bag
Two pieces of plain sashiko fabric 11 x 8½in (27.9 x 21.6cm) for outside panels
Two pieces of plain cotton 11 x 8½in 27.9 x 21.5cm) for lining

For the red bag
Two pieces of red striped fabric 9½ x 8½in (24.1 x 21.6cm) for outside panels
One piece of red *tsumugi* cotton 4 x 8½in (10.2 x 21.6cm) for base panel
One piece of plain cotton, 22 x 8½in (60 x 21.6cm) for lining

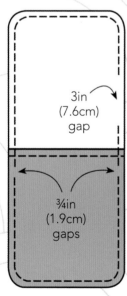

BLUE BAG

① **Marking and stitching the sashiko:** Mark and cut curved bottom corners on the outside panels and the lining using a 2½in (6.4cm) diameter circle template. Zigzag the edges of the sashiko fabrics to prevent fraying.

② Select a sashiko pattern of your choice, mark it (page 22) and stitch the sashiko (page 25). *Nowaki* and *seigaiha* were drawn on a 1in (2.5cm) grid with a 2in (5.1cm) diameter circle template, plus a 1½in (3.8cm) template for *seigaiha* inner curves, with the top row echoed in variegated thread. Lightly press the finished sashiko from the wrong side.

③ **Making the bag:** Assemble the bag using ¼in (6mm) seams throughout. With right sides together, sew one outside panel to one lining piece across the top only (**Fig 1**) and press the seam towards the outside panel. Repeat with the second panel and lining piece but this time press the seam towards the lining piece.

④ With right sides together, outer against outer and lining against lining, sew the bag together (**Fig 2**). Sew to 1in (2.5cm) below the top of the bag, to create a frilled effect when the bag is closed. Remember to leave ¾in (1.9cm) gaps unsewn for the drawstring, shown by arrows on the diagram, and a 3in (7.6cm) gap unsewn in the lining. Press seams open and clip seam allowances to ⅛in (3mm) around corner curves.

⑤ Turn the bag right side out, through the lining gap. Push the lining down inside the bag and press. Mark two lines across the bag, joining the ends of the gaps left for the drawstring, 1in (2.5cm) and 1¾in (4.4cm) from the top edge. Stitch around the bag on each line to make a channel for the drawstring. Insert each drawstring, knot the ends and slipstitch the lining gap closed. To add the decorative flowers to the ends of the drawstring, follow the instructions in the panel on page 51.

Fig 1

Fig 2

3in
(7.6cm)
gap

¾in
(1.9cm)
gaps

One side of the blue bag uses the seigaiha *variation pattern, as seen here, while the other side features the* nowaki *pattern (shown top left).*

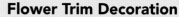

RED BAG

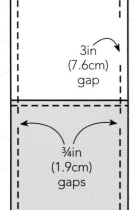

1 **Marking and stitching the sashiko:** Select a sashiko pattern, mark it (page 22) and then stitch the sashiko (page 25). I used the width of the woven stripe in the fabric to work *matsukawabishi* and *kagome*. *Komezashi* was worked on a ⅜in (1cm) grid in two colours on the base panel. Lightly press the finished sashiko from the wrong side.

2 **Making the bag:** Assemble the bag, using ¼in (6mm) seams throughout. With right sides together, sew one outside panel to a base panel (**Fig 1**) and press the seam towards the outside panel. Repeat with the second panel.

3 With right sides together, sew the bag outer to the lining piece across the top only. Press one seam towards the bag outer and the other seam towards the lining piece. Fold the bag so the outer fabric is right sides together, the outer/lining seam lines up and the lining is right sides together and then sew the bag side seams (**Fig 2**). Sew to 1in (2.5cm) below the top of the bag to create a frilled effect when closed. Remember to leave ¾in (1.9cm) gaps unsewn as indicated by the arrows, for the drawstring, and a 3in (7.6cm) gap unsewn in the lining. Press seams open.

4 To finish your red bag, refer back to step five of the blue bag.

Flower Trim Decoration
These traditional trims finish off the drawstrings neatly and attractively.

1 Fold one 3½in (8.9cm) square of cotton in half, right sides together, and sew a ¼in (6mm) seam to make a tube. Press the seam open.
2 Turn half of the tube right side out, so the fabric is doubled and the seam allowance hidden. With a double length of sewing thread, run small running stitches around the raw end of the tube.
3 Slip the tube over the knotted end of the drawstring (with raw ends towards the knot) and gather up tightly (**Fig 3**). Take a few stitches through the cord and knot to finish off. Fold the tube down over the knot so it is hidden inside.
4 For optional 'stamens' use yellow sashiko thread. Pinch the open end of the tube to flatten it and stitch thread through at the creases and leave loose. Pinch the end the other way and stitch another thread through. Hold all four ends of thread and knot together close to the end of the tube. Trim thread ends to finish.

Fig 1

This side of the red bag uses *kagome* with *komezashi* below, while the other side (shown top left) features *matsukawabishi* with *komezashi* below.

Fig 2

3in (7.6cm) gap

¾in (1.9cm) gaps

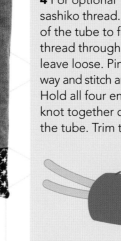

Fig 3   gather here

ZABUTON CUSHIONS

Zabuton (floor cushions) are used in Japan when people sit on *tatami* (mats made of straw and rush) and are especially important for comfort when sitting around the sunken *irori* hearth. The borders on my floor cushions echo the *irori* fender. The *kiku* (chrysanthemum) motifs are based on old *furoshiki* (wrapping cloths). Real *zabuton* are squarish rectangles but mine are designed to use a 20in (50.8cm) square cushion pad. Choose thick cotton furnishing fabric for the cushion back.

Sashiko patterns used
Fan cushion – *kawari sayagata* page 91
Flower cushion – *komezashi* page 97
Finished size of cushion 20in (50.8cm) square

You will need

For each cushion
Butter muslin 21in (53.3cm) square

Fine sashiko thread (exact quantity depends on sashiko pattern selected)

Thick dark blue cotton 18in (45.7cm) square, for cushion back

18in (45.7cm) zip

Basic sewing and marking kit (see page 16)

Sewing machine

For the fan cushion
Blue *tsumugi* cotton 15½in (39.4cm) square, for centre

Four pieces of *tsumugi* or other striped/checked cotton 18½ x 3½in (47 x 8.9cm), for border

Black polyester wadding (batting) 21in (53.3cm) square

Medium variegated sashiko thread

For the flower cushion
Checked fabric 15½in (39.4cm) square, for centre

Four pieces of *tsumugi* or other striped/checked cotton 18½ x 3½in (47 x 8.9cm), for border

Fine green sashiko thread

Variegated perlé thread No.8

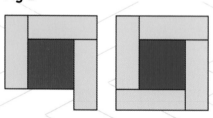

FAN CUSHION

1 **Making the cushion front panel:** Machine sew one of the striped border pieces to the cotton you are using for the centre square, using a ¼in (6mm) seam allowance. Sew only half the seam for the first piece, as shown in **Fig 1** left. Sew the remaining border pieces to the centre piece, going back to finish the first seam after sewing on the others, as shown in **Fig 2**. Press the seams towards the border pieces.

2 **Marking and stitching the sashiko:** Choose a marking method (see page 22) and mark the sashiko pattern as shown in **Fig 3a** (below). Layer the cushion top, muslin or wadding (batting) and backing (see tacking fabric layers, page 22). Stitch the sashiko, working the fan motif first, stitching each petal outline individually, beginning at the top and stitching towards the cushion corner. Finish with the threads on the front at the corner, plaiting these threads together when the fan is finished (see picture, right).

3 Stitch the *kawari sayagata* background pattern with one strand of thread. Finally, work rows of running stitch along the border stripes.

4 **Making up the cushion:** Use ½in (1.3cm) seams throughout. Place the front panel and backing fabric right sides together and machine or tack (baste) across the bottom edge. Machine sew 1½in (3.8cm) at the beginning and end of the tacking (basting), starting and finishing with a few backstitches. Press the seam open. From the wrong side, tack (baste) the zip in place (making sure the zip pull is facing the right way to open your cushion from the outside!). With the zip foot on the sewing machine, sew the zip in place. Check the zip opens properly and then remove tacking. With the zip open, place the other three edges of the quilted panel and backing together and machine sew all round with a ½in (1.3cm) seam allowance. Clip the corners, turn right side out and press the seam. Insert the pad to finish.

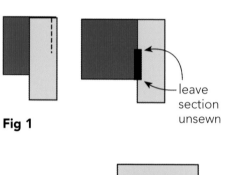

Fig 1

leave section unsewn

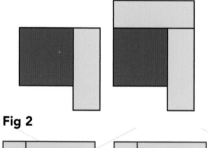

Fig 2

Fig 3a Fan motif

To draw the fan motif, draw lines 12½in (31.8cm) long from one corner. Mark the first line at a 45-degree angle by folding the square diagonally and marking along the fold line, then add more lines to divide the fan into eight equal sections. Link the ends of the lines to form an arc. Complete the fan using a 2½in (6.4cm) circle template to mark the inner and outer petals. Draw remaining lines along the centre of each petal. Use a 6in (15.2cm) circle template to mark a circle segment in the corner. Mark the background area with a 1 x ½in (2.5 x 1.3cm) diagonal grid for *kawari sayagata* or another pattern of your choice.

Idea
Adapt the overlap cushion back method on page 38 if you prefer not to use a zip. For a floor cushion, you will need to slipstitch the open back closed or it will open up in use. Using a doubled medium or thick thread, you can add traditional corner and centre thread tassels too – see panel page 55.

FLOWER CUSHION

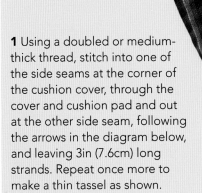

Fig 3b Flower motif

To draw the chrysanthemum flower motif, mark the exact centre of the cushion front. Draw lines 11in (27.9cm) long crossing over the centre to divide the circle into 16 equal sections. Mark the 45 degree diagonal lines by folding the square diagonally and marking along the fold line, first one way then the other, and add more lines to divide the flower. Use a 2½in (6.4cm) circle template to mark the central circle. Referring to the picture above, complete the flower by marking the inner and outer petals around the flower using 2in (5.1cm) and 2½in (6.4cm) circle templates. Draw remaining lines along the centre of each petal.

❶ Making the cushion front panel: Machine sew one of the striped border pieces to the checked fabric you are using for the centre square, using a ¼in (6mm) seam allowance. Sew only half the seam for the first piece, as shown in **Fig 1** opposite on page 54. Sew the remaining border pieces to the centre piece, going back to finish the first seam after sewing on the others, as shown in **Fig 2** on page 54. Press the seams towards the border pieces.

❷ Marking and stitching the sashiko: Choose a marking method (see page 22) and mark the sashiko pattern as shown in **Fig 3b**, left. Layer the cushion top and muslin backing or wadding (batting) and backing (see tacking fabric layers, page 22). Stitch the sashiko, starting with the flower motif. Stitch the petals in sequence, starting at the centre and working outwards around the top of a petal. Strand across the back to stitch along the adjacent outer petal, back to the centre along the petal centre line and repeat all around the flower.

❸ Stitch the *komezashi* (rice stitch) background with one strand of your sashiko thread, using the fabric pattern as a grid. Use variegated cotton perlé No. 8 for the diagonal stitches on half the centre panel, to give the illusion that the background square is split into two triangles.

❹ Making up the cushion: Follow step 3 for the fan cushion opposite to make up the flower cushion.

Adding Traditional Corner Tassels

For a traditional look to your zabuton floor cushions you could add some simple corner tassels in a toning or contrasting thread.

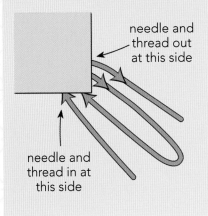

1 Using a doubled or medium-thick thread, stitch into one of the side seams at the corner of the cushion cover, through the cover and cushion pad and out at the other side seam, following the arrows in the diagram below, and leaving 3in (7.6cm) long strands. Repeat once more to make a thin tassel as shown.

2 Tie all the strands together in a single knot, loosely at the corner, as shown in the picture above and then trim the thread ends.

needle and thread out at this side

needle and thread in at this side

MOYŌZASHI TABLE RUNNER

A table runner is a good project for a sashiko sampler. I used five patterns as five is a lucky number in Japan but you could add more. The central sashiko was worked as embroidery, with a muslin layer added before stitching the straight lines in the border. *Kawari asanoha* (hemp leaf variation) begins the strip. *Ganzezashi* (sea urchin stitch) appears twice, as the basic pattern (lower end) and turned through 45-degrees with extra lines (second from top). With *yatsude asanoha* (eight-lobed hemp leaf) near *ganzezashi*, it is easy to see how the two patterns relate. *Shippō tsunagi* (linked seven treasures) has the grid lines and diagonal lines also stitched (centre). Red diagonal lines divide the patterns and the diagonal grid common to all is stitched in brown, with a single red line in each pattern.

Sashiko patterns used (top to bottom)
Kawari asanoha page 73, *ganzezashi* and variation page 66, *yatsude asanoha* page 67 and *shippō tsunagi* page 64

Finished size of table runner 41 x 13½in (104 x 34.3cm)

You will need

- Sashiko fabric 34½ x 7in (87.6 x 17.8cm)
- Two pieces of striped *tsumugi* cotton 34½ x 5in (87.6 x 12.7cm)
- Two pieces of striped *tsumugi* cotton 5 x 15in (12.7 x 38.1cm)
- Butter muslin 43 x 15in (109 x 38.1cm)
- Plain black cotton 42½ x 15in (108 x 38.1cm), for backing
- Fine sashiko thread in various colours (exact quantity depends on patterns selected)
- Basic sewing and marking kit (see page 16)
- Sewing machine

Idea

Try using different sashiko designs for your table runner. Look for patterns that share the same base grid or can be turned or distorted to fit (see distorting patterns page 21).

❶ Marking and stitching the sashiko: Select the sashiko patterns of your choice. All the patterns on my runner were based on a 1½in (3.8cm) grid and the full design is shown in **Fig 1**. Zigzag the edges of the sashiko fabric to prevent fraying, then mark the patterns and stitch the sashiko. Lightly press the finished sashiko from the wrong side.

❷ Assembling the central panel: With right sides together, machine sew one 34½ x 5in (87.6 x 12.7cm) piece of striped cotton to the side of the sashiko panel, using a ½in (1.3cm) seam. Sew the second piece to the opposite side. Press seams outwards. Machine sew the 5 x 15in (12.7 x 38.1cm) pieces of cotton to either side of the central panel, using ½in (1.3cm) seams. Press seams outwards. Tack (baste) the muslin to the back of the panel and

then stitch the lines of sashiko in the border through both layers (see tacking fabric layers, page 22).

❸ Making up the runner: Place the front panel and backing fabric right sides together and pin all round. Machine sew with a ½in (1.3cm) seam allowance, leaving an 8in (20.3cm) gap at the centre of the lower edge. Trim off the corners within the seam allowance, but do not cut right up to the stitches – to about ⅛in (3mm). Bag out the runner, i.e., turn it the right way out through the unsewn gap. Ease the corners out so they are nice and sharp. Lay the runner flat and smooth it out. Turn under the raw edges at the bottom of the runner, pin or tack (baste) and slipstitch the gap closed. From the back, sew right around the whole panel ¼in (6mm) from the edge with small, neat hand stitches through the backing and seam allowances only, to keep the backing in place.

Fig 1

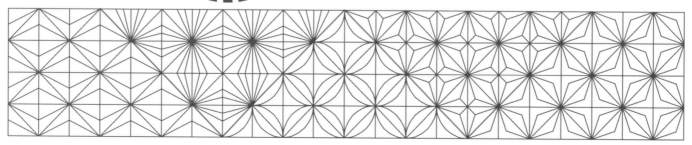

56

PATTERN LIBRARY

This Pattern Library contains over 100 sashiko patterns for you to experiment with and is divided into *moyōzashi* (pattern sashiko) (pages 58–91) and *hitomezashi* (one stitch sashiko) patterns (pages 96–109). They are all traditional. Patterns like *raimon* (lightning spiral) and *yatsude asanoha* (eight-lobed hemp leaf) are taken from antique sashiko garments, while others such as *shippō tsunagi* (linked seven treasures) have endured as popular designs. For many of the *hitomezashi* patterns, it is the first time they have appeared in an English language book. See page 127 for a complete index of all the patterns.

MOYŌZASHI SASHIKO PATTERNS

These designs have curved or straight lines of running stitch which change direction to make larger patterns. The *moyōzashi* patterns in this library are arranged in related groups beginning with the easiest and progressing in a logical sequence. The groups also start with the easiest, spirals and squares, working up to maze-like key patterns. If you are new to sashiko, try to resist the temptation to jump in at the deep end!

MOYŌZASHI STITCHING TIPS

- In *moyōzashi*, pattern lines cross but the stitches do not.
- Count the stitches in the short pattern sections for nice, even sashiko.
- When turning corners, make the last stitch right into the corner so the pattern is sharply defined (see page 25).
- Where pattern lines meet, space the stitches so they don't touch each other.
- Where indicated in some pattern diagrams by red dashed lines, strand loosely across the back of your work, as shown below, and when making a sharp change of direction, leave a little loop on the back for ease.

The patterns are presented as individual stitched samples, with the stitching sequence shown in an accompanying diagram. The stitched samples are colour coded to help you follow a traditional stitching sequence, as this is not only the easiest and most economical way but will also produce the neatest results.

The diagrams show the grids in blue and the stitching lines in black. However, where a grid line is stitched as part of the pattern, only the black stitching line appears (the blue being hidden by the stitching) e.g., the vertical lines in *asanoha* (hemp leaf, page 72). The stitching direction is shown by red arrows with a red dot for the starting point. The use of circle templates is indicated by tinted circles. Red dashed lines indicate where thread should be stranded loosely across the back of the work. See also page 20 for drawing patterns using grids.

Grid Measurements
The grids for the following *moyōzashi* patterns are based on imperial measurements but are easy to convert to metric using the following formula:
    To convert inches to centimetres,
    multiply the measurement in inches by 2.54,
    e.g., 2in x 2.54 = 5.08cm
See page 20 for commonly used imperial-metric conversions in this book.
You could round grid measurements up or down for easiest metric marking.

right: This sashiko sampler quilt features all 60 dark blue *moyōzashi* samples, bordered with striped *tsumugi* cotton. Individual samples were stitched through one layer and the finished quilt layered with black wadding (batting) before extra quilting was added. Size: 84 x 67in (213 x 170cm).

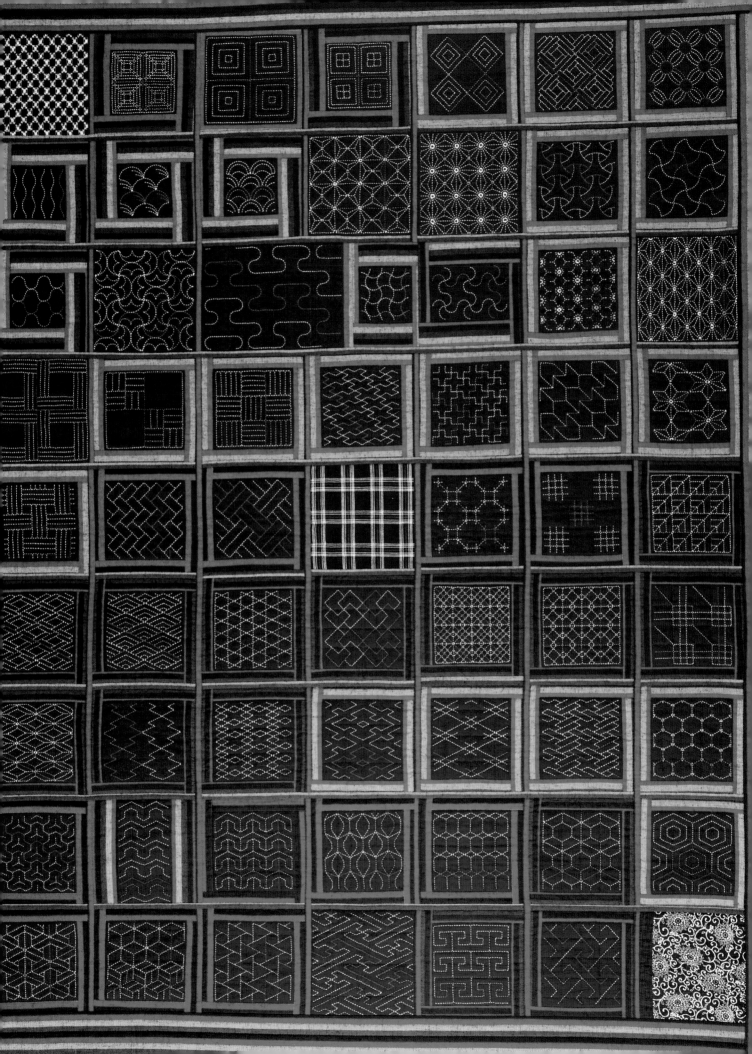

SPIRALS IN SQUARES

Some of the oldest surviving sashiko pieces have patterns from this group. Early sashiko stitchers would have used the coarse weave of the fabric to align their stitches. Once the basic foundation grid has been completed with straight lines, each square is filled in by stitching in a spiral direction. Keep your stitches as even as possible on the long straight lines, but don't count them for evenness – there are too many!

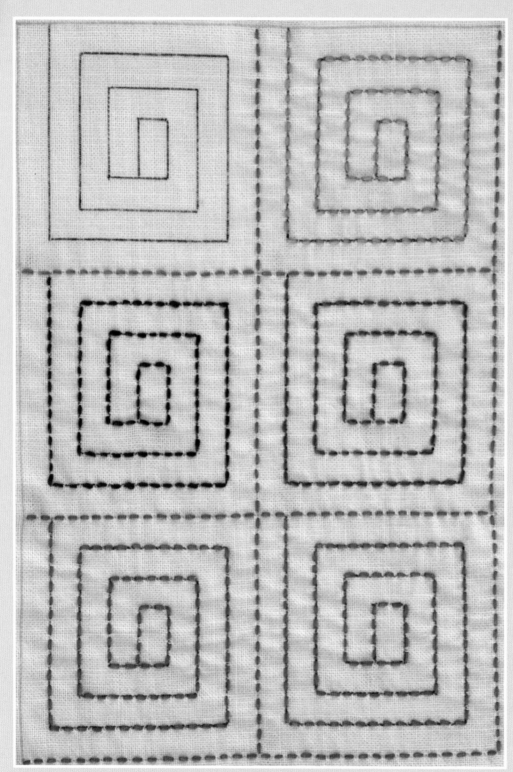

Raimon *pattern*

Spirals and concentric squares have been used in Japanese design since prehistoric times.

Raimon or inazuma
(lightning spiral)

This is an ancient pattern. *Hanten* (short jackets) were stitched with raimon or *masuzashi* (shown below), often with very large designs covering half the width of the garment, in combinations of squares and rectangles. It is easy to resize it to suit your project.

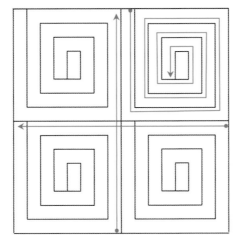

Mark a grid – the sample is 3in. Mark individual spirals with lines at $3/8$in intervals. From the top and following the red arrows, stitch vertical lines (shown in red on the stitched sample), then stitch horizontal lines (shown in light brown). Stitch each spiral individually (shown in yellow, green and dark brown).

Masuzashi
(square measure sashiko)

This looks like the nesting wooden boxes once used to measure out rice, sake and other goods. Nowadays, sake shops use the smaller size to serve a taste and the cedar wood enhances the sake's flavour. The different sizes are said to represent the household labour contribution made by men (large measure), women (medium) and children (small). A secondary pattern of squares on point appears where the pattern tessellates.

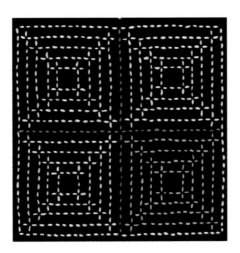

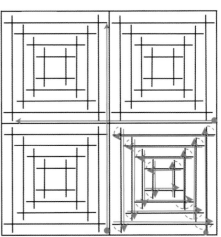

Mark a grid – the sample is 2½in. Mark nesting squares at ¼in intervals, including corner crosses. Following the red arrows, stitch vertical lines (red), then horizontal lines (light brown). Stitch each nest of squares individually (yellow), spiralling towards the centre. Cross the corners of each square by one stitch, stranding across the back, indicated in the diagram by red dashed lines.

Idea

For a more elaborate version of *masuzashi* seen in old sashiko, try crossing the corners over the preceding square or, on a larger starting grid, alternate crossed corners with plain right angles. Sometimes the little loops at the corners, normally on the back, are formed on the front.

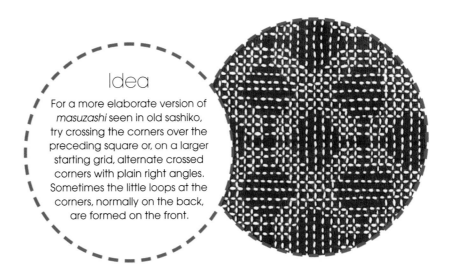

Hiratsume sanmasu
(three concentric squares)

This has the same stitch sequence as *masuzashi* but without the overlapping corners. It is also a repeat of the *mimasu kamon* (three measures family crest) used by the family line of famous Kabuki actor Ichikawa Danjuro XII (Kabuki names are handed down through the generations).

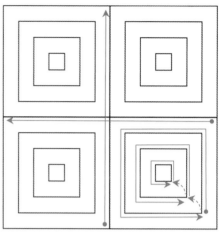

Mark a grid – the sample is 3½in. Mark nesting squares at ½in intervals. Following the red arrows, stitch vertical lines (red), then horizontal lines (light brown). Stitch each nest of squares individually (yellow), spiralling towards the centre and stranding across the back, indicated in the diagram by red dashed lines.

Tsumeta
(boxed rice fields)

This is derived from the kanji character *ta* (rice field), shown below. You could work the same pattern on a diagonal grid to make *miedasuki* (triple crossed 'tasuki' cord), with four diamonds in the centre (see distorting patterns, page 21).

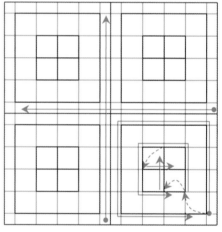

Mark a grid – the sample is ½in, with 2½in large squares. Mark 2in and 1in squares within the large squares. Mark a cross through the centre square. Following the red arrows, stitch vertical lines (red), then horizontal lines (light brown). Stitch each nest of squares individually (yellow), spiralling towards the centre and stranding across the back, indicated in the diagram by red dashed lines. Finish by stitching the central crosses.

Tip

With practise, once the large grid is marked, the spirals or squares can be stitched without extra marking if you can stitch straight parallel lines! Spirals within squares and rectangles were popular for old sashiko because they were so easy. Along with simple step designs (see *dan tsunagi*, page 74) they are known as *kagizashi* (hook or key sashiko). *Kaginote* means a 'right angled bend'.

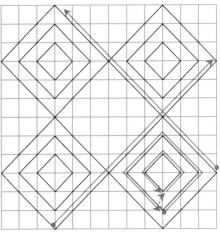

Tatemimasu
(three upright squares)

This turns the *hiratsume sanmasu* motif through 45 degrees and alternates it with plain squares. Three is a lucky number in Japan. Five and seven are also lucky. The famous *Shichigosan* (seven, five, three) festival celebrates childrens' healthy growth, at age 3 and 5 for boys and 3 and 7 for girls.

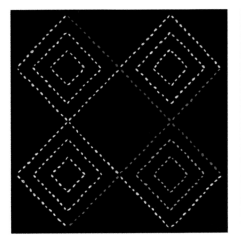

Mark a grid – the sample is ½in. Mark diagonal lines, then nesting squares at ½in intervals. Following the red arrows, stitch diagonal lines (red and light brown). Stitch each nest of squares individually (yellow), spiralling towards the centre and stranding across the back, indicated in the diagram by red dashed lines.

Kumiko
(lattice)

This is reminiscent of the intricate woodwork on sliding *shoji* doors, backed with translucent white paper and used to create flexible living space in traditional Japanese homes. The individual strips of wood, beautifully jointed to create the trellis patterns, are called *kumiko*. Overlapping corners echo the *manji*, a Buddhist symbol (see *hishi manji* pattern, page 83).

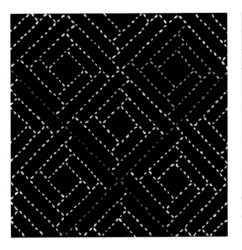

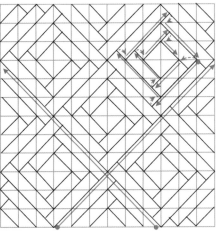

Mark a grid – the sample is ½in. Mark the main diagonal lines, then individual pattern squares at ½in intervals. Following the red arrows, stitch the diagonal lines (red and light brown). Stitch each pattern square individually (yellow), spiralling towards the centre and stranding across the back.

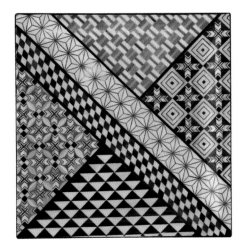

Yosegi marquetry, a speciality of Hakone, near Tokyo, uses many designs also seen in sashiko. Patterns on this small tray include (clockwise from the top): *hirasan kuzushi* variation (page 76), *tatemimasu* variation (top of this page), *asanoha* page 72, *ishidatami* page 103, *urokozashi* page 104 and a variation of *shippō tsunagi* page 64.

CIRCLES AND CURVES

The circles in these patterns are an illusion – they are all stitched with intersecting curves! After marking a basic grid, a compatible circle template is all you need to draw the complete design. *Shippō tsunagi* (linked seven treasures) is probably the best known of this group and in the past was stitched in many parts of Japan. It is also called *shippō* (seven treasures). These patterns are also seen on kimono for the *Nōh* drama, appearing as backgrounds to scattered leaves, flowers or auspicious motifs woven in rich brocades.

Shippō tsunagi
(linked seven treasures)

This was one of various *yūsoku* patterns used by courtiers since the Heian era, nearly a thousand years before it appeared in sashiko (*yūsokukojitsu* are the ancient practices and rituals of the Imperial Court). Sometimes the pattern was filled in with imaginary flowers called *wachigai* (crossed circles), which was forbidden to commoners. You may also recognize it as the quilting pattern Wineglass or from Roman mosaics. The seven treasures appear in Buddhist sutras (religious texts) and are gold, silver, lapis lazuli, agate, pearl, coral and crystal but there are no groups of seven in the pattern. It may be a pun on *shihō* (four directions or four sides).

Mark a grid – the sample is 1in. Use a 2in circle template to mark the interlocking circles (shown in blue on the diagram). Following the red arrows, stitch diagonal wavy lines (shown in red on the stitched sample). Work around the pattern in a continuous line (shown in light brown and yellow).

Maru shippō
(circular seven treasures)

This pattern has doubled diagonal wavy lines and circles where they cross. The circle is a positive image in Japan and a symbol of the sun. The sun goddess Amaterasu Oumikami is the principal deity of the Shinto religion, and, of course, the sun symbol is on the national flag. *Maru batsu* (indicating a circle or cross with your arms above your head) is a way of signing right and wrong or true and false. *Maru* can also mean 'whole' or 'complete'.

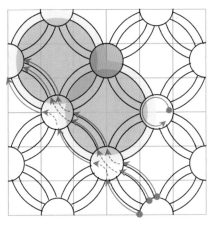

Mark a grid – the sample is 1in. Use a 3in circle template (shown in pale blue on diagram) to mark *shippō tsunagi*, left. Use a 2½in circle template to mark a circle within each circle (shown in mid blue) and 1in circle template to mark circles at the pattern intersections (in pink). Following the red arrows, stitch separate 1in circles first (red). Stitch diagonal wavy lines (light brown, yellow, green and cream), working around the pattern in continuous lines and stranding across the back.

Fundō
(scale weights)

This is also called *fundō tsunagi* (linked scale weights) and is half *shippō tsunagi* – only one wavy line is stitched on each diagonal. The shape of traditional scale weights tessellate to make the pattern. Wealthy *daimyō* (feudal lords) had gold ingots cast in the same symmetrical shape.

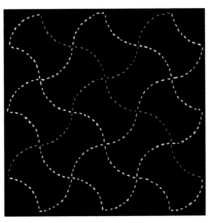

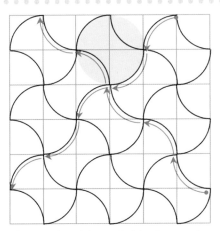

Mark a grid – the sample is 1in. Use a 2in circle template (shown in blue) to mark wavy lines. Following the red arrows, stitch diagonal wavy lines (red and light brown).

Maru bishamon
(circular 'Bishamon' pattern)

This is one of several patterns from the armour scales of the Buddhist guardian deity Bishamonten. He is depicted as a warrior carrying a *hōtō* (treasure tower), bringing courage, prosperity and protection from demons and is associated with the colour blue. Two more *bishamon* patterns are on pages 88 and 89. To mark *maru bishamon* in other sizes, use a circle-to-line-spacing ratio of 5:3, i.e. use a 5in circle with 3in line spacing.

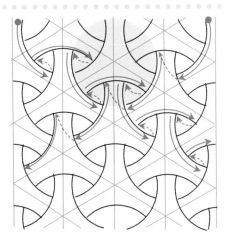

Mark vertical lines at 1½in intervals. Use the 60 degree line on a quilter's ruler to draw an isometric grid. Use a 2½in circle template to mark interlocking circles (shown in blue). Following the red arrows, stitch curved segments in a diagonal direction (red and light brown), working in continuous lines and stranding across the back. Stitch remaining curved segments in the other diagonal direction (yellow).

DIAMOND STARS

To non-Japanese, these patterns may look like stars. They are all based on an angular version of *shippō tsunagi* (see page 64), with curves replaced with zigzag lines. The simplest version is known as *hishi shippō* (diamond seven treasures) and is stitched in the same sequence as the *shippō* variation. *Ganzezashi* (sea urchin stitch) is the main decorative pattern used on Tobishima, an island off the coast of Shonai in northern Japan. The extra diagonal lines give an illusion of complexity but it is easy to stitch.

Ganzezashi *pattern*

Hishi shippō is the alternate name for the top half of this pattern sample. Extra lines for a more complex version (shown right, with diagram) are marked in black on the lower half, with the inner lines elegantly curved.

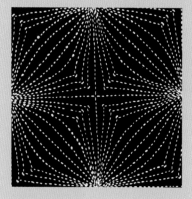

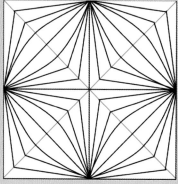

Ganzezashi
(sea urchin stitch)

This is also called *uni* (sea urchin). *Ganze* is a dialect word. Fishing is the main occupation on the island of Tobishima and *uni* are a delicacy. The pattern expresses hopes for a good catch. The basic *ganzezashi* diagonal unit was often stitched as a band alternating with a large stepped pattern, one of several designs called *yamagata* (mountain form or shape).

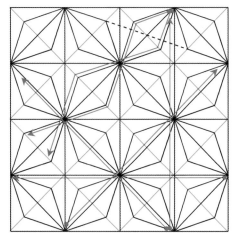

Mark a grid – the sample is 1½in. Mark diagonal lines. Mark the zigzag lines using the dashed line in the diagram (top right) as a guide. Following the red arrows, stitch vertical lines (shown in red on the stitched sample opposite). Stitch horizontal lines (shown in light brown) and then the diagonal lines (yellow and light green). Work the zigzags in a continuous line (dark brown and dark green).

Yatsude asanoha
(eight-lobed hemp leaf)

This is a further development of the simplest *hishi shippō* design. The base grid is rotated through 45 degrees and the sides of neighbouring diamond shapes are linked with a cross. The *yatsude* plant's Latin name is *Fatsia japonica*, called the castor oil plant in Britain. Its large leaves look exotic but it is very hardy and popular all over Japan. The pattern was thought to ward off evil and looks like an octagonal version of *asanoha* (hemp leaf, page 72). The all-over version shown here is from a *donza* (fisherman's coat) in Fukuoka City Museum. The variation is adapted from a design from Hokusai's *Shingata Komoncho* (New Forms of Small Patterns Book), 1824. As the variation is half of the full design, the instructions are given first. If you want to stitch a large pattern area, cut a diamond-shaped template to speed up marking.

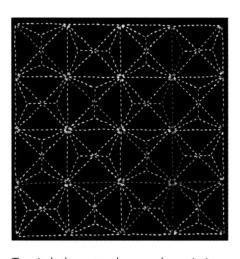

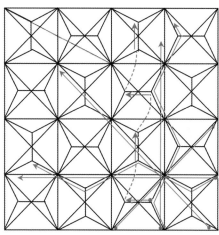

To stitch the *yatsude asanoha* variation, mark a grid – the sample is 1½in. Mark the diagonal lines. Mark zigzag lines using the dashed line in the diagram (top) as a guide. Following the red arrows, stitch the vertical lines (red), then the horizontal lines (light brown) and diagonal lines (yellow and light green). Stitch zigzags in a continuous line (rust and pink). Finally, stitch short horizontal and vertical lines, stranding across the back, indicated in the diagram by red dashed lines.

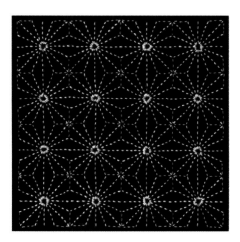

To stitch the full *yatsude asanoha* design, mark a grid and follow the instructions for the variation above, but also mark and stitch all zigzag lines (shown in cream). Stitch short vertical and horizontal lines (red and light brown), keeping thread continuous and stranding across the back.

WAVES

Waves and wavy lines characterize the following patterns. Like the circle and curve designs, they take a little more time to mark but are easy to stitch, especially *seigaiha* and *nowaki*. The six remaining designs are stitched in continuous lines, with no stranded threads on the back, making them suitable for two-sided items. Wave patterns were often used to strengthen the corners of old *furoshiki* (wrapping cloths).

Seigaiha *pattern*
Seigaiha and its variation (opposite) are based on a simple clamshell pattern, which is easy to mark and stitch in various sizes.

Seigaiha
(blue ocean waves)

This pattern became fashionable in the mid 18th century. Old coins from the Akita Prefecture (northern Honshu) have this design on the back. *Seigaiha* remains very popular in Japan, decorating all kinds of items from paper to ceramics. Designs representing water are especially appreciated during the humid summer, when they give a feeling of coolness.

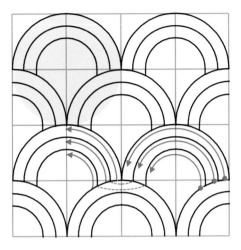

Mark a grid – the sample is 1in. Use circular templates with diameters of 2in, 1½in and 1in to mark the arcs. Following the red arrows in the diagram, stitch the largest arcs first (shown in red on the stitched sample opposite), working in rows. Then stitch the middle (brown) and centre (yellow) arcs, working in rows and stranding across the back (shown in the diagram by red dashed lines).

Seigaiha variation

This differs from the basic pattern by replacing the innermost curve with a shallow arc, which gives a sophisticated look. It makes an elegant design used as a background for scattered motifs of falling cherry blossoms or maple leaves, as seen on kimono fabrics of the Edo era (1615–1868). The pattern has been used on the blue drawstring bag on page 50.

 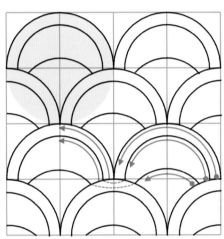

Mark a grid – the sample is 1in. Use circular templates with diameters of 2in and 1½in to mark the arcs. Use the same stitching sequence as *seigaiha* above (red, brown, yellow).

Nowaki
('grasses')

This literally translates as a 'wintry blast' or 'searing autumn wind', and the kanji character *no* can mean 'wild'. Devastating typhoons are a regular feature of autumn weather in Japan. In a legend of the Heian era (794–1185), the morning after a typhoon revealed rice and grasses bent right over by the wind. The pattern is usually called 'grasses' in English. Use it to give a seasonal reference to your sashiko. I have used it on one side of the blue drawstring bag on page 49.

 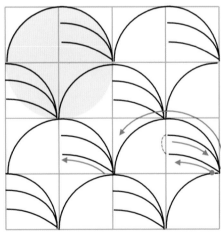

Mark a grid – the sample is 1in. Use a 2in diameter circle template to mark the arcs. Use the same template to mark the curved 'grasses'. Following the red arrows, stitch across the row. Stitch the lower grass first, strand across back to stitch the upper grass and finally stitch across the arc. Repeat to the end of the row.

Tatewaku
(rising steam)

These wavy lines decorate ancient Buddhist statues and textiles in the Shōsoin Imperial repository at Nara. Like *shippō*, page 64, it was often shown with motifs such as clouds or flowers, filling the design spaces.

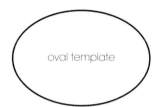

 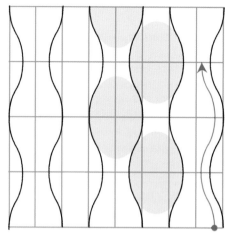

Mark a grid – the sample is 1in x ½in. Use a 1½in long oval template (provided left) to draw the curves. Following the red arrow, stitch the individual curved lines.

Amimon
(fishing nets)

This is often realistically depicted in designs featuring everyday items, either whole fishing nets hanging up to dry or the shape as an all-over pattern like the version shown here. Fishing nets are an auspicious motif and many Japanese festivals and traditions in coastal areas have their origins in the hopes of a great catch.

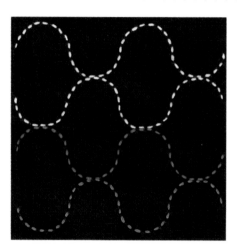 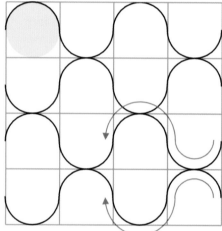

Mark a grid – the sample is 1in. Use a 1in diameter circle to draw the curves. Following the red arrows, stitch the wavy horizontal pattern lines.

Hanmaru tsunagi
(linked semicircles)

This is much easier than it looks! Two sets of *amimon* curve at right angles to each other to form large curves; the double arcs are stitched afterwards. The pattern can be traced back to ancient Roman mosaics, where the shape represented Amazonian shields.

Mark a grid – the sample is 1in. Use a 2in diameter circle to draw the large curves and a 1in diameter circle to draw the small double arcs. Following the red arrows, stitch the large horizontal curves (red) and large vertical curves (light brown). Stitch small double arcs as continuous lines, horizontal first (yellow) then vertical (green).

Kasumi tsunagi
(linked mist)

This originates in Heian art, when naturalistic images rather than stylized imaginary landscapes were popular with the nobility. By the Edo era (1615–1868), *kasumi* was established as a decorative device, used to divide designs as well as being used an all-over pattern.

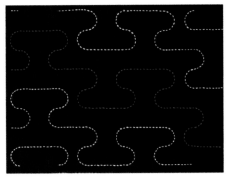 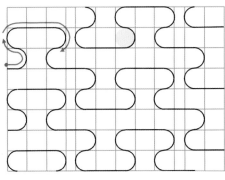

Mark a grid – the sample is 1in, with every sixth column marked as ½in. Use a 1in diameter circle template to draw the curves. Following the red arrows, stitch the individual pattern lines.

Toridasuki
(crossed birds)

This looks like the simplified shapes of two birds (*tori*) linked by a cross over (*dasuki*). The *tasuki* is also a length of cord or fabric, looped over the shoulders and crossing in the middle of the back, into which kimono sleeves are tucked, so they are out of the way while working.

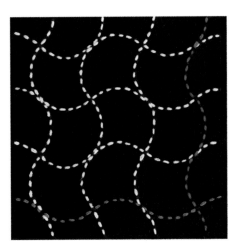 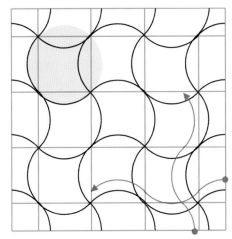

Mark a grid – the sample is 1in. Use a 1½in diameter circle to draw the curves. Following the red arrows, stitch vertical pattern lines (red), then horizontal pattern lines (brown).

Chidori tsunagi
(linked plovers)

This may represent either the shape of the birds themselves, fitting together like a jigsaw, or the flock's meandering flight. The plover is a common bird in Japan and its cute, simplified image appears as a scattered motif in many patterns.

 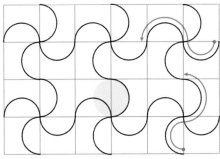

Mark a grid – the sample is 1in. Use a 1in diameter circle to draw the curves. Following the red arrows, stitch the vertical pattern lines (red) first, then the horizontal pattern lines (brown).

HEMP LEAF

Star-like *asanoha* (hemp leaf) is probably the most famous sashiko pattern. It originally came from China, where it was associated with Buddhism and represented radiating light or even the inner light of the soul. Before cotton became available to ordinary people, hemp was a very important source of cloth. There are many *asanoha* variations. It was particularly popular for children's clothes and bedding, and clothing for newborn babies would be decorated with the design in the hope that the child would grow up strong, like the hemp plant. It also symbolized a wish for good health.

Asanoha
(hemp leaf)

This pattern may be worked in any size. It is easier to stitch if you do not mark the shallow vertical zigzags until *after* you have stitched the main vertical lines and the large zigzag lines. Take care not to let your stitches cross on the front where the pattern lines intersect. The little gaps build up to make a rosette effect in the leaf centres.

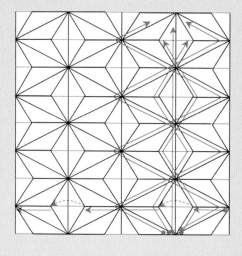

Mark a grid – the sample is 1½in. Divide squares horizontally into rectangles. Use the grid as a guide to mark the large zigzag lines. Do *not* mark the rest of the pattern at this stage. Following the red arrows, stitch the vertical lines (shown in red on the stitched sample). Then stitch the diagonal lines as zigzags, forming figures of eight (shown in light brown and yellow). Mark and stitch shallow vertical zigzags, also as figures of eight (dark brown and dark green). Finally, stitch the short horizontal lines (turquoise), keeping thread continuous and stranding across the back (red dashed lines on diagram).

Kuzure asanoha
(fragmented hemp leaf)

This resembles the blurred patterns of *kasuri* ikat fabrics. Follow the same stitching instructions and diagram as *asanoha*, left, but only sew the first two stitches in each section. The sample threads have been changed – rust, light green and pink replace dark brown, dark green and turquoise in the instructions. Using a variegated thread also produces a fragmented effect (see the jacket on page 115).

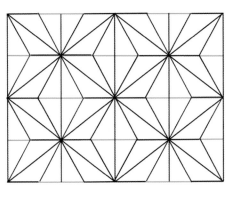

Tip

When marking the shallow vertical zigzags, don't attempt to line up with the midpoint of the horizontal lines; instead, the angle at the top of the shallow vertical zigzag should be equal between the vertical line and the large zigzag. When stitching smaller versions of this pattern, it is easier to 'eyeball' the line and stitch without marking. Use the length of your needle against the fabric to determine the line.

Kawari asanoha
(hemp leaf variation)

This is a distorted version of the original *asanoha* pattern. The design is stretched vertically and is less dense than the original. By changing the proportions of the base grid, as shown in the diagram (right), you can make vertical adjustments to the design to fit your project (see the long samplers on page 26).

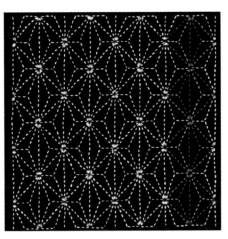

Mark a square grid – the sample is 1in. Do not divide the grid further before marking the pattern. Continue to mark and stitch, following instructions for *asanoha*.

Tobi asanoha
(scattered hemp leaf)

This pattern also appears in Islamic art. It is quite a difficult variation, with a different stitching sequence and you will need to mark the whole pattern before starting to stitch. As some of the short horizontal lines are quite a long way apart (shown in turquoise in the sample), you will need to stitch them individually, rather than stranding from one to the next. If combining *tobi asanoha* with hexagon patchwork, use a 60/30-degree set square to draw the pattern based on an isometric grid.

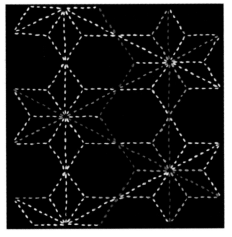

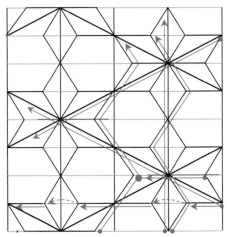

Mark a grid – the sample is 1½in. Divide the squares horizontally into 1½ x ¾in rectangles. Using the grid as a guide, mark diagonal lines and shallow vertical zigzag lines. Following the red arrows, stitch vertical lines (red), then diagonal lines (light brown and yellow), then shallow vertical zigzags (rust and green). Stitch horizontal lines (pink), keeping thread continuous and stranding across the back (red dashed lines in diagram). Stitch short horizontal lines individually (turquoise).

STEPS AND WEAVES

Patterns from everyday man-made objects are all around in Japanese homes and gardens and have inspired many designs for textiles and paper. Traditional buildings have beautiful details made of woven bamboo and even thin strips of wood, used for ceilings and panels. In the modern world, it is easy to forget that arrow feathers and well curbs were once everyday objects.

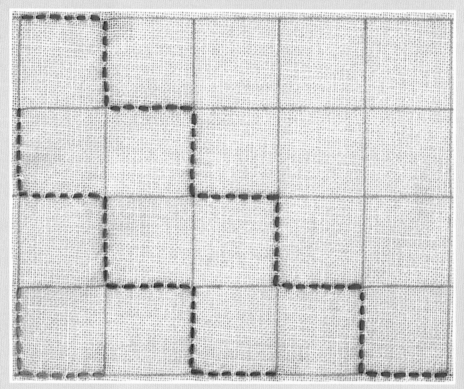

Dan tsunagi
(linked steps)

This is a very easy design and quick to stitch. On coarsely woven cloth or on checks, the fabric threads could be used to line up the pattern. When the spaces between the steps are filled in with more identical rows of steps, one of several patterns called *yamagata* (mountain form) is created. The Chido Museum, Tsurouka City, Yamagata, has several *hanten* (jackets) stitched with *yamagata* and sampler squares of different stitches. It is a versatile design.

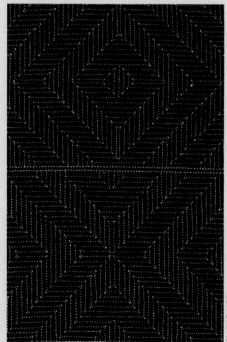

CHIEKO HORI

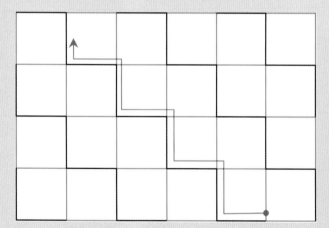

Mark a grid – the sample is 1in. Following the red arrows, stitch the steps (shown in in red, light brown and yellow on the stitched sample above).

Yabane
(arrow feather)

This pattern is based on a *dan tsunagi* foundation. There are many designs based on arrows, a symbol of warriors from ancient times. Some of the earliest are on items stored at the Shōsoin Imperial Repository. Archery contests, including those on horseback, form part of various festivals. Families display miniature armour and arrows on Children's Day on 5 May and at New Year, a lucky white-feathered arrow called *hamaya* is sold at temples.

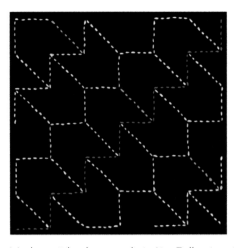 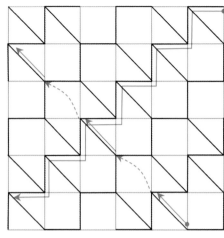

Mark a grid – the sample is 1in. Following the red arrows, stitch the step pattern (red). Then stitch short diagonal lines (light brown), keeping the thread continuous and stranding across the back, indicated in the diagram by red dashed lines.

Jūjitsunagi
(linked '10' crosses)

This pattern is named after the kanji character for ten, which is written as a cross (see below). It suggests prosperity, with ever increasing tens. The shape is made from two sets of steps creating a tessellated puzzle.

 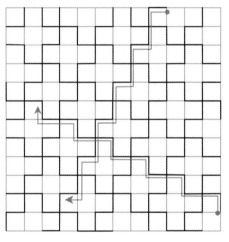

Mark a grid – the sample is ½in. Following the red arrows, stitch the stepped pattern (red). Then stitch the remaining steps (light brown).

Nanamehōgan tsunagi
(diagonal linked crosses)

This is stitched in the same way as *jūjitsunagi* but on a diagonal grid. It works well within diagonal shapes and with other diamond patterns.

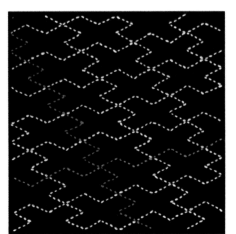 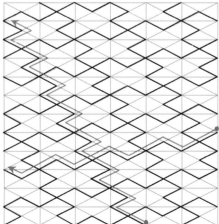

Mark a grid – the sample is 1 x ½in diagonal grid. Following the red arrows, stitch the stepped pattern (red). Then stitch the remaining steps (light brown).

Gokuzushi
(simple five form)

Five is a lucky number in Japan and this pattern based on five lines has a subtle woven effect. I adapted this version of *gokuzushi* from origami paper, using a stitching sequence based on other sashiko designs. *Kuzushiji* means the simplest form of kanji character, written with one straight line.

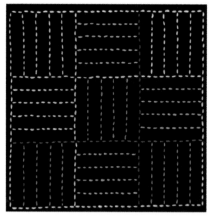

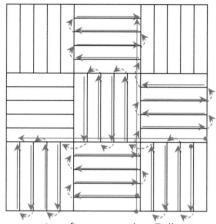

Mark a grid – the sample is 2in. Mark each square into five rectangles. Following the red arrows, stitch vertical then horizontal lines (red and light brown). Fill in each square, alternating vertical and horizontal line infills (yellow and green).

Hirasan kuzushi
(simple three lines form)

This pattern alternates plain squares with groups of four smaller squares. It is stitched in a similar sequence to *gokuzushi* above. Three is another lucky number!

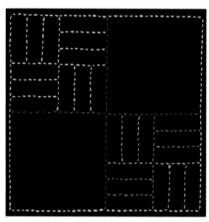

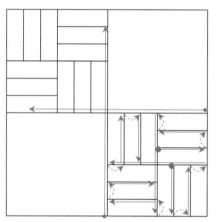

Mark a grid – the sample is 3in. Quarter alternate squares, to make four 1½in squares. Divide each square into three rectangles. Following the red arrows, stitch vertical then horizontal lines (red and light brown). Fill in large squares individually: fill in small squares stitching outwards from the centre line, back on the line above, then the centre line – reversing this order at the end of the centre line (yellow). Finish the large square by stitching the other two smaller squares in the same way (green).

Igeta koshi
(well curb check)

This is the first of several sashiko patterns using the kanji '*i*' (well), the shape of the well curb or guard. Fashionable *kasuri* ikat were often patterned with *igeta* and other sashiko designs use this motif (see *igeta ni hakkaku tsunagi* and *hirai jūmon*, page 79).

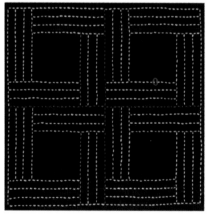

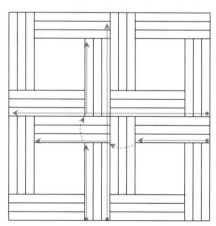

Mark a grid – the sample is 4in. Mark a border inside each square, 1in deep, with parallel lines along each border section. Following the red arrows, stitch vertical then horizontal lines (red and light brown). Stitch remaining lines vertically (yellow), keeping thread continuous and stranding across the back. Stitch horizontal lines the same way.

Ishidatami
(paving block)

This pattern shows an arrangement of paving stones, although it also looks like the kind of woven ceiling patterns made from thin strips of wood. It is also called *sankuzushi* (simple three form) and is very easy to stitch. The checkerboard pattern, called *arare* (hailstone) in *yūsoku* textiles (used by the Imperial Court), is also called *ishidatami* (see pattern, page 103).

 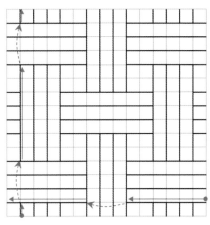

Mark a grid – the sample is ⅜in. Following the red arrows, stitch vertical lines first, keeping thread continuous and stranding across the back, indicated in the diagram by red dashed lines. Finish by stitching horizontal rows the same way (light brown), taking care not to stitch through the vertical strands on the back.

Higaki
(cypress fence)

This is easy to stitch, despite looking complicated. *Higaki* panels make beautiful backgrounds to plants in Japanese gardens. The pattern is also popular for *rinzu*, a plain-coloured woven silk damask, which is dyed by various techniques for women's formal kimono.

 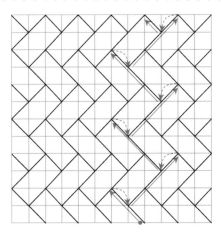

Mark a grid – the sample is ½in. Use the grid as a guide to mark diagonal pattern lines. Following the red arrows, stitch the pattern in vertical sections, keeping thread continuous and stranding across the back.

Ajiro
(wickerwork)

This pattern is similar to *ishidatami* (top of page) at first glance, but there are just two divisions to each rectangle and the pattern is rotated through 45 degrees. The pattern is also stitched in a different sequence. It is reminiscent of Japanese woven gates and fences.

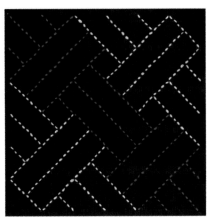 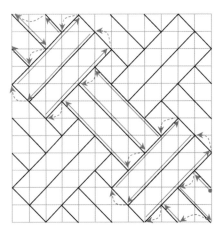

Mark a grid – the sample is ½in. Use the grid to mark the diagonal pattern lines. Following the red arrows, stitch the pattern in diagonal sections, keeping thread continuous and stranding across the back.

SQUARES

This group of designs reflects a Japanese passion for plaids and *kasuri* ikat, which have been popular since the mid Edo era (1615–1868). As woven designs, plaids offer almost limitless possibilities and might include variegated effects or pre-dyed threads left over from *kasuri*. As a way of using up remnants of thread from other projects, plaids (along with stripes) were the mainstay of many country weavers well into the 20th century. In contrast, hand woven *kasuri* is very time consuming and therefore expensive. Sashiko offers an alternative way to achieve a similar look.

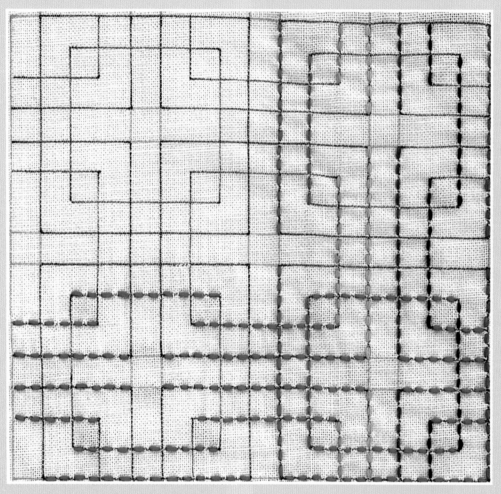

Kakuyose
(intersecting square corners)

This is the kind of geometric pattern popular for men's *yukata* (cotton kimono), along with Kabuki 'riddle plaids' (where pattern elements are puns on actors' names) and sumo wrestlers' named patterns. This is another design that looks complicated but isn't; it has square-within-square motifs superimposed. Although I marked the pattern on the grid for the cream sample piece, you can stitch the pattern straight on to a grid, without further marking.

Mark a grid – the sample is ⅜in. Following the red arrows, stitch vertical lines first, keeping thread continuous (shown in red, yellow, light green, dark green and light brown on the stitched sample) and stranding across the back, indicated in the diagram by red dashed lines. Finish by stitching the horizontal rows in the same way (all shown in red), taking care not to stitch through the vertical strands on the back.

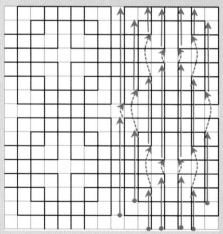

Igeta ni hakkaku tsunagi
(special linked well curbs)

This pattern combines octagons and squares (see *igeta koshi* for more information, page 76). The well curb motifs are stitched individually and this design would look good stitched in two colours.

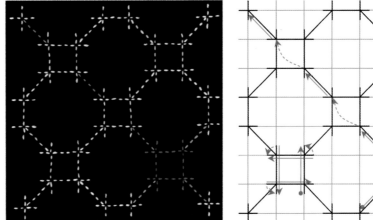

Mark a grid – the sample is ¾in. Following the red arrows, stitch *igeta* motifs individually first, keeping the thread continuous within each motif and stranding across the back, indicated in the diagram by red dashed lines. Finish by stitching the diagonal lines (light brown and yellow), keeping thread continuous and stranding across the back, as before.

Hirai jūmon
(crossed well curb)

This has a double *igeta* motif, just like a *kasuri* ikat pattern. Each motif is stitched individually. The sample motif is stitched in red.

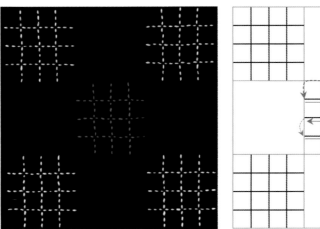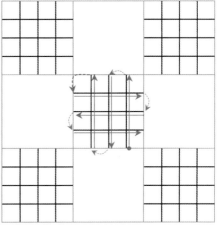

Mark a grid – the sample is 2in. Mark alternate squares with a ½in grid. Following the red arrows, stitch the vertical lines first, keeping the thread continuous and stranding across the back, indicated in the diagram by red dashed lines. Finish by stitching the horizontal rows the same way, taking care not to stitch through the vertical strands on the back.

Tip
When turning corners, be sure to make the last stitch right into the corner, so the pattern will look sharp and well defined.

Tsumiki
(building blocks)

This combines squares and diagonals in an interesting pattern. Although the pattern is fairly dense, it is quite straightforward to stitch.

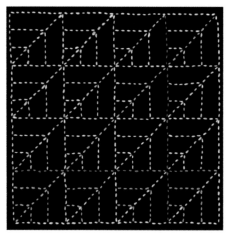 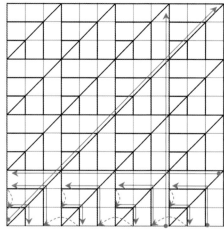

Mark a grid – the sample is ½in. Mark diagonal lines at 1½in intervals, sloping up towards the right. Following the red arrows, stitch vertical lines first (red), then horizontal lines (light brown) and diagonal lines (yellow). Fill in each square, stitching around the corner and back again (green), keeping thread continuous and stranding across the back.

Koshi tsunagi
(linked check)

This is another square and diagonal combination, with a more open design. Unless the pattern is stitched on a smaller scale, you will need to stitch the second half of the square outline individually. For a variation, stitch each square separately and omit the diagonal lines.

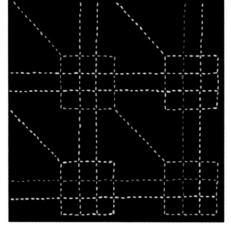 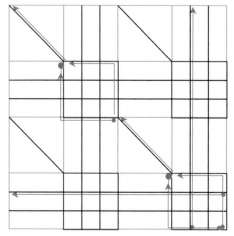

Mark a grid – the sample is 1½in. Mark extra vertical and horizontal lines at ½in intervals as shown in the diagram. Mark the diagonal lines, as shown. Following the red arrows, stitch the vertical lines first (red), then stitch the horizontal lines (light brown). Stitch around half of each square and along the diagonal line to link to the next square, keeping the thread continuous (yellow). Finish by stitching around the other half of each square individually (green).

Idea

Checks, plaids and simple square trellis designs adapt easily for sashiko. You could try designing a new sashiko pattern from a favourite textile or decorative object.

Hiyoku igeta
(double or paired well curb)

This pattern turns the *igeta* motif through 45 degrees to link with the next motif (see *igeta koshi* for more information, page 76). Add diagonal lines to the pattern and it becomes *kasane masu tsunagi* (layered linked measuring boxes), pictured below.

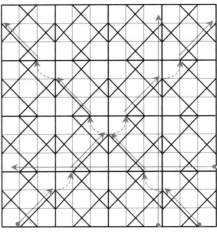

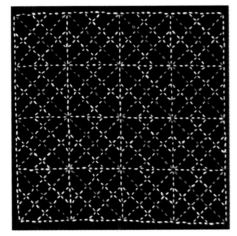

Mark a grid – the sample is ½in. Mark *igeta* motifs using the grid as a guide. Following the red arrows, stitch vertical lines at 1½in intervals first (red), then horizontal lines (light brown). Stitch diagonal lines in one direction (yellow), keeping the thread continuous and stranding across the back. Finish by stitching the diagonal lines in the other direction (green), taking care not to stitch through vertical strands on the back.

Hiragumi manji tsunagi
(linked manji)

This is based on a Buddhist symbol. *Manji* are found in temples and on Buddhist art, and are even used on maps to mark temple locations. It originates in ancient India, where it has a common origin with the swastika but with a completely different use and meaning. *Manji* signify the source of life and the universe and symbolize the Chinese concept of Yin and Yang, with the central cross reflecting the power that gives birth to everything. The *hiragumi manji tsunagi* pattern also resembles the well-known modern patchwork block, Card Trick.

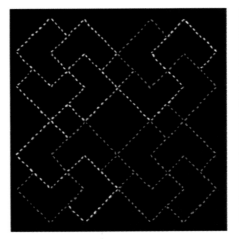

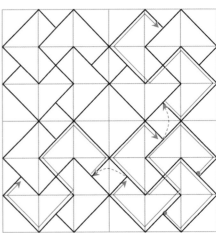

Mark a grid – the sample is 1in. Mark the diagonal pattern lines using the grid as a guide. Following the red arrows, stitch the pattern in vertical sections, keeping thread continuous and stranding across the back. Finish by stitching the pattern in horizontal sections, as before (light brown).

DIAMONDS

Like many *yūsoku* patterns used by the Imperial Court, the basic *tasuki* (diamond-shaped lattice) pattern dates from the Heian era (794–1185). They are also called *hishi*, which literally means 'water chestnut', after the shape of its leaves and fruit. Do you see lattices or the shapes inside? The diamond shape, like the folding fan, is associated with expansion, so diamond patterns can symbolize a wish for increase. Various diamonds also feature in many *kamon* (family crests).

Hishi moyō
(diamond pattern)

This forms the basis for all the patterns in this section, whether the stitches form continuous lines, broken lines or a varied shape. To mark each diagonal grid, start with a rectangular grid on a 2:1 ratio and fill it with diagonal lines. Each pattern gives an appropriate grid size. (See also varying the grids, page 21.)

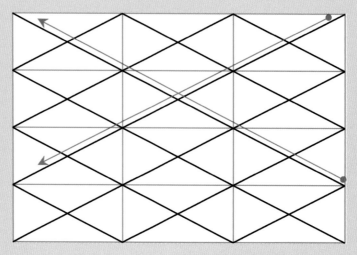

Mark a grid – the sample is a 1 x 2in diagonal grid. Following the red arrows, stitch diagonal lines in one direction (shown in red, light brown, yellow and green on the sample) and then the other direction (dark brown).

Kagome
(woven bamboo)

In Japan, woven bamboo remains indispensable for everyday activities. Bamboo is an extraordinary raw material, growing more quickly than wood and capable of being fashioned into many useful items. Bamboo baskets would have been a very familiar item at the time this pattern was first stitched in sashiko. The pattern uses *hishi moyō* diagonal lines with vertical lines stitched first.

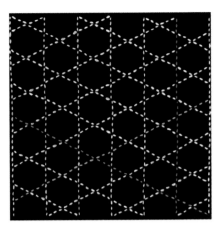

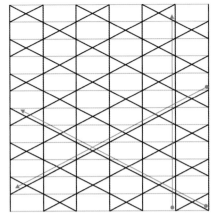

Mark a grid – the sample is a 1 x ½in diagonal grid. Following the red arrows, stitch vertical lines (red). Stitch the diagonal lines as for *hishi moyō*, opposite.

Hishi seigaiha
(diamond blue waves)

This is an interesting variation on the original *seigaiha* pattern (page 68). There are several possible stitch sequences. The one shown right is my favourite, as it seems to be the most economical for thread!

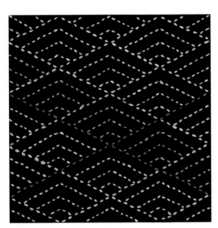

Mark a grid – the sample is a ⅜ x ¾in diagonal grid. Following the red arrows and instructions for *hishi moyō* opposite, stitch diagonal lines to form a grid with diamonds 3in wide (red and light brown). Fill in each diamond, back and forth (yellow), keeping thread continuous and stranding across the back.

Hishi manji
(diamond manji)

This easy-to-stitch pattern uses the same Buddhist *manji* symbol as its base as *hiragumi manji tsunagi* (page 81).

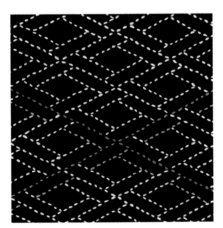

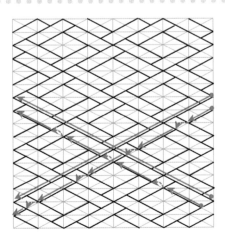

Mark a grid – the sample is a ⅜ x ¾in diagonal grid. Following the red arrows and instructions for *hishi moyō* opposite, stitch diagonal lines to form a grid with diamonds 3in wide (red and light brown). Stitch remaining diagonal lines (yellow and green), keeping thread continuous and stranding across the back.

Sanjū hishi tsunagi
(three linked diamonds)

This has elongated hexagons as part of the pattern. It is another design based around threes, for good luck.

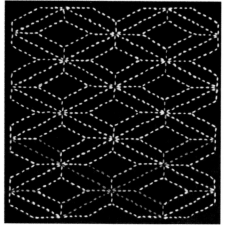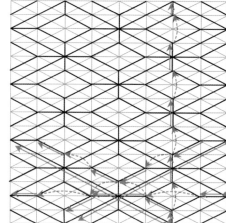

Mark a grid – the sample is a ⅜ x ¾in diagonal grid. Following the red arrows and instructions for *hishi moyō* (page 82), stitch diagonal lines to form a grid with diamonds 3in wide (red and light brown). Stitch vertical and horizontal lines (yellow and green), keeping thread continuous and stranding across the back. Stitch remaining diagonal lines (rust and pink).

Matsukawabishi
(pine bark diamond)

This was especially popular in the Momoyama era (1568–1615) and Edo era (1615–1868), when it was used for *kosode* (the forerunner of modern kimono) and *Nōh* drama costumes. It is a quick pattern to stitch. Pine represents long life and good fortune. It may be represented by boughs, needles or by more abstract designs.

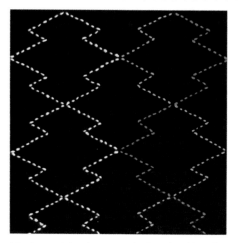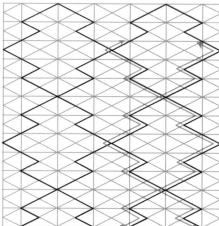

Mark a grid – the sample is a 1 x ½in diagonal grid. Following the red arrows, stitch the pattern in continuous lines (red and light brown).

Yotsugumi hishi
(four interlaced diamonds)

This is stitched with intersecting diagonal lines, although it looks like individual linked motifs. It is similar to *takedabishi* (see page 106), the family crest of the feudal lord Takeda – a diamond quartered into adjoining small diamonds by two crossing lines.

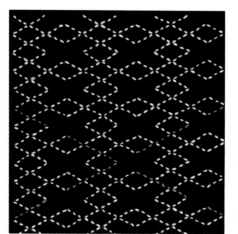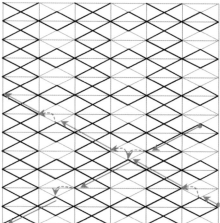

Mark a grid – the sample is 1 x ½in diagonal grid. Following the red arrows, stitch diagonal lines (red and light brown), keeping thread continuous and stranding across the back.

Idowaku
(diagonal well curb)

This is another design using the *igeta* motif (see *igeta koshi* page 76 for more information). As each unit is stitched individually, this gives the option for using different thread colours in the pattern.

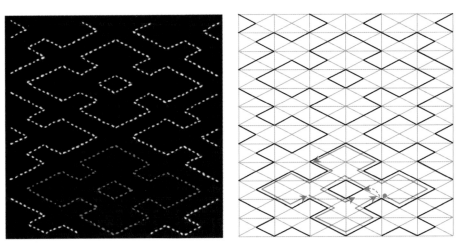

Mark a grid – the sample is a 1 x ½in diagonal grid. Following the red arrows, stitch around each individual motif (red), keeping the thread continuous and stranding across the back.

Hishi igeta
(well curb diamond)

This resembles *kasuri* ikat fabrics and is stitched like *yotsugumi hishi* (opposite). If stitched with continuous diagonal lines, the same pattern becomes *tasukimon* (crossed sash or diamond lattice pattern).

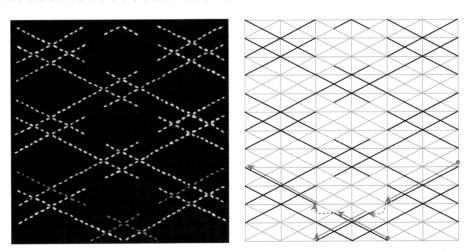

Mark a grid – the sample is 1 x ½in diagonal grid. Following the red arrows, stitch the diagonal lines (red and light brown), keeping thread continuous and stranding across the back.

Kumi hishi
(interlaced diamond)

This is a more difficult pattern. Check the stitched sample and the diagram frequently to make sure the gaps in the diagonal lines are the right length – some lines have a gap of one diagonal unit, others have a gap of two units, depending on where they are in the pattern. The interlaced diamonds appear as the second diagonals are completed.

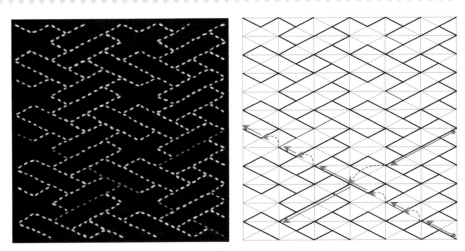

Mark a grid – the sample is a 1 x ½in diagonal grid. Following the red arrows, stitch the diagonal lines (red and light brown), keeping thread continuous and stranding across the back.

HEXAGONS

In Japan, the hexagon is called *kikkō*, meaning 'tortoiseshell'. It is used as an abstract reference to the tortoise, a symbol of a long life and happiness. According to legend, when a tortoise reaches 1000-years old, it is able to speak human language and foretell the future. It is often paired with the crane (another symbol of longevity). Objects in the Shōsoin Imperial Repository dating from the Nara era (645–794) are decorated with hexagons but the motif became really popular from the Heian era (794–1185) onwards. *Kikkō* is used to decorate many things, with many pattern variations. It looks different from traditional English hexagon patchwork patterns because *kikkō* hexagons point upwards. The patterns in this section are traditionally stitched on a diagonal grid but can also be worked on an isometric grid if you prefer (see varying grids, page 21).

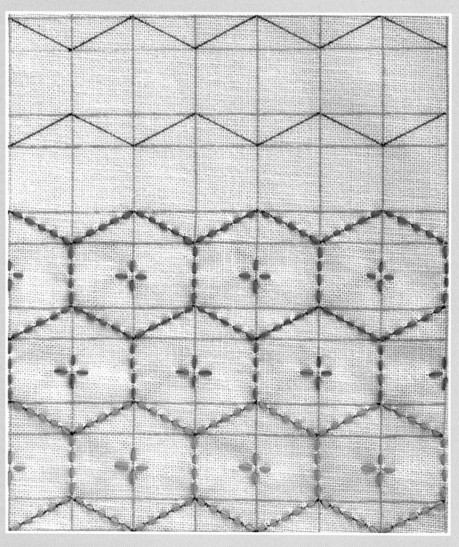

Jūji kikkō
(cross tortoiseshell)

This pattern continues the tradition of filling in the hexagon with a floral centre. Some of the Shōsoin designs include filled hexagons, usually with an imaginary four-petalled flower, sometimes called *karabana* (Chinese flower). The sashiko pattern is worked in rows. Draw extra horizontal lines (optional) to keep the centre crosses straight.

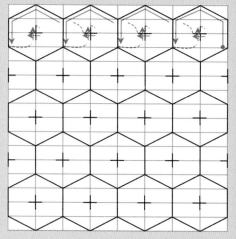

Mark a grid – the sample is ⅜ x ¾in. Mark diagonal lines to form the tops of the hexagons. Following the red arrows, stitch the pattern in rows, stitching around three sides of the hexagon (shown in red on the stitched sample), keeping the thread continuous and stranding across the back to stitch the centre crosses, indicated in the diagram by red dashed lines.

Tsuno kikkō
(horned tortoiseshell)

This has overlapping stitches where pattern lines intersect, similar to *masuzashi* (page 61). On a larger scale, without the overlaps and with inner hexagons, it becomes *kikkō* (shown below).

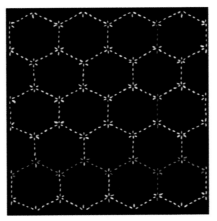

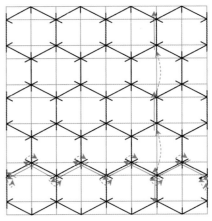

Mark a grid – the sample is ⅜ x ¾in. Mark diagonal lines for tops of hexagons. Following the red arrows, stitch vertical lines (red), keeping thread continuous and stranding across the back to cross each line by one stitch. Stitch horizontal zigzag lines (light brown), keeping thread continuous and stranding as before.

Arare kikkō
(hailstone or segmented tortoiseshell)

This *kikkō* pattern has two sizes of hexagon superimposed on top of one another.

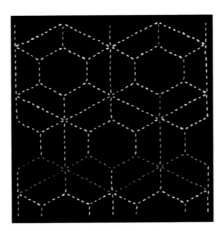

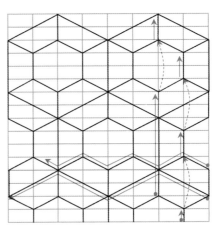

Mark a grid – the sample is a ⅜ x ¾in diagonal grid. Following the red arrows, stitch horizontal zigzag lines (red). Stitch smaller zigzag lines (light brown) then short vertical lines (yellow), keeping thread continuous and stranding across the back. Stitch longer vertical lines (green) keeping thread continuous, as before.

Nijū kikkō tsunagi
(double linked tortoiseshell)

This is another hexagon within a hexagon pattern, but this time the centre hexagon is turned on its side and elongated.

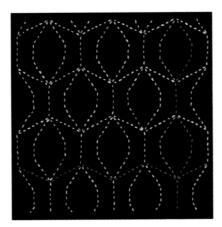

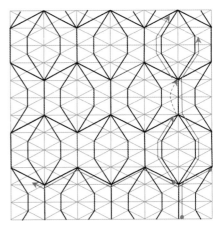

Mark a grid – the sample is a ½ x 1in diagonal grid. Mark the short vertical pattern lines. Following the red arrows, stitch horizontal zigzag lines (red), then vertical lines, following the hexagon shape (light brown). Stitch remaining vertical sections (yellow), keeping thread continuous and stranding across the back.

Kasane kikkō
(layered tortoiseshell)

This pattern is also known as *kikkō hishi tsunagi* (linked diamond tortoiseshell). Do you see the pattern as overlapping hexagons or long hexagons with diamonds? The latter gives a better clue as to how it is stitched – as horizontal lines of diamonds, linked with vertical lines to make the pattern.

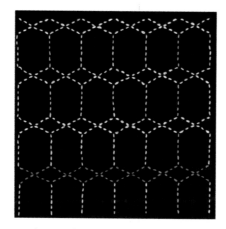 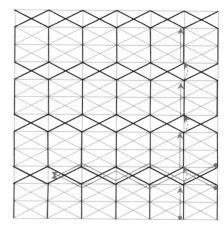

Mark a grid – the sample is a ½ x 1in diagonal grid. Following the red arrows, stitch the first horizontal zigzag lines (red), then the second horizontal zigzag lines (light brown). Stitch remaining vertical sections (yellow), keeping thread continuous.

Mukai kikkō
(facing or alternate tortoiseshell)

This pattern fragments the basic *kikkō* design and is often used as a background to other motifs. Stitched without the vertical lines, it is known as *yamagata* (mountain form) (below).

 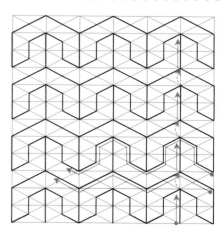

Mark a grid – the sample is a ½ x 1in diagonal grid. Following the red arrows, stitch vertical sections (red), keeping thread continuous and stranding across the back. Stitch horizontal zigzag lines (light brown). Finish by stitching the horizontal stepped line, following the pattern (yellow). To stitch the *yamagata* pattern (shown left), omit the vertical lines.

Bishamon kikkō
(Bishamon tortoiseshell)

This represents the armour scales of the Buddhist deity Bishamonten, one of the *Shichifukujin* (seven gods of good luck), said to bring fortune and good health (see also *maru bishamon*, page 65). They are a popular New Year image, often depicted on *takarabune* (treasure ship), sailing in from the sunrise. Each scale is made up of three *kikkō* – three being a lucky number.

 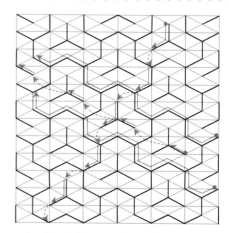

Mark a grid – the sample is a ½ x 1in diagonal grid. Following the red arrows, stitch the continuous stepped diagonal lines (red and light brown). Stitch the short stepped lines (yellow), keeping thread continuous and stranding across the back. Stitch the short diagonal lines (green), keeping thread continuous as before.

Yosegi
(mosaic or parquetry blocks)

This resembles the patchwork pattern Tumbling Blocks. *Yosegire* is traditional mosaic marquetry. Strips of exotic woods are glued together in patterns and cut into thin slices. The veneer is used to decorate items such as a *himitsu-bako* (personal secret box), a puzzle opened by sliding the side panels in a special order (see also the marquetry picture on page 63). These patterns have recently been used for patchwork quilts. The top of the sashiko sample has been left unfinished to make *hakozashi* (box stitch).

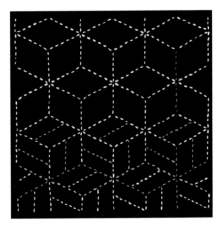 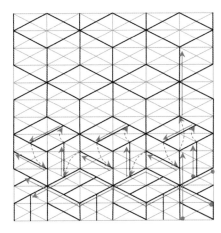

Mark a grid – the sample is a ½ x 1in diagonal grid. Following the red arrows, stitch vertical lines (red), then horizontal zigzag lines (light brown and yellow). Finish by stitching the remaining angled lines (green), keeping thread continuous and stranding across the back.

Musubi kikkō
(connected tortoiseshell)

This looks like a real puzzle to stitch! *Musubi* also means 'knot' and knotted ropes called *shimenawa* (written as '7-5-3 rope') are used to mark off sacred areas like shrines or to confine spirits in trees or rocks. *Musubi kikkō* combines triangles and *kikkō*, so you are stitching lucky threes with longevity! The pattern is built up with broken diagonal lines, so it is fairly easy to work – just remember where the gaps are and strand across the back of the fabric, like stitching *kumi hishi* (page 85).

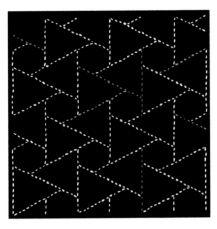 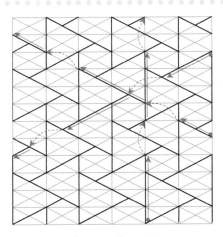

Mark a grid – the sample is a ½ x 1in diagonal grid. Following the red arrows, stitch vertical lines (red), then diagonal lines (light brown and yellow), keeping thread continuous and stranding across the back.

Kawari bishamon kikkō
(Bishamon tortoiseshell variation)

This extends the three short lines in the centre of the armour scale to make a triangular grid. The pattern gives an illusion of an endless weave.

 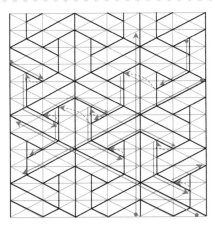

Mark a grid – the sample is a ½ x 1in diagonal grid. Following the red arrows, stitch the vertical lines (red), then diagonal lines (light brown and yellow). Stitch the short angled lines (green), keeping thread continuous and stranding across the back. Stitch remaining angled lines (rust), keeping thread continuous.

KEY FORMS

Key or fret patterns look complex and resemble mazes. *Sayagata* is named after a kind of brocade weave. It was introduced to Japan from China during the Muromachi era (1392–1568). Trading relations had been re-established after Zen was introduced to Japan in the Kamakura era (1185–1392) and Japanese monks travelled abroad regularly. Chinese designs made a big impact with the aristocracy at this time. *Sayagata* is thought to have been introduced to China along the Silk Road from ancient Greece and it certainly looks like many Greek key patterns. It is a good background for scattered motifs. It is also called *rinzu*, and is a popular pattern for the woven silk damask used for women's formal kimono.

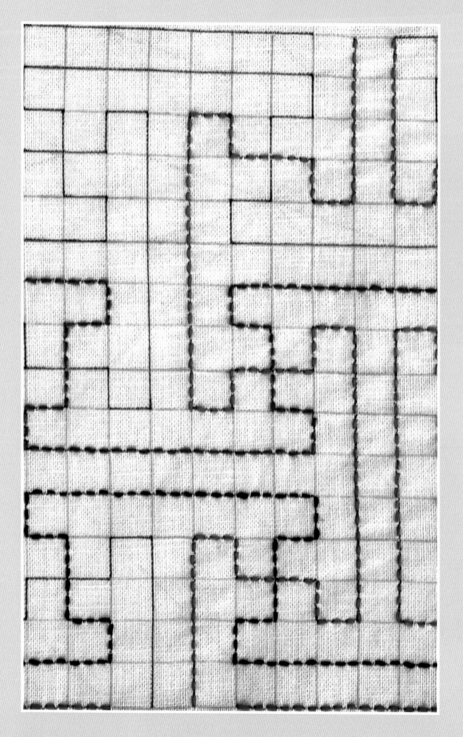

Sayagata
(saya brocade pattern)

This looks like a maze but it is easy to follow the design. The stitching forms continuous lines and changes direction frequently. Once you have marked a basic grid, work your way around the pattern. It is a good idea to keep a picture of *sayagata* in front of you while you work.

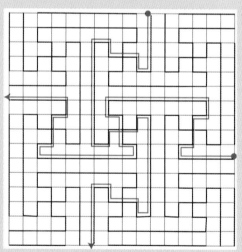

Mark a grid – the sample is ½in. Following the red arrows, stitch the vertical lines, changing direction around the pattern (shown in red and light brown on the stitched sample). Then stitch the horizontal lines (shown in dark green, dark brown and rust).

Kawari sayagata
(sayagata variation)

This is the same pattern as *sayagata* but is stitched on a diagonal grid. It is also called *hishi sayagata* (diamond sayagata).

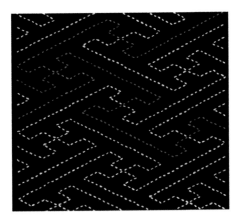 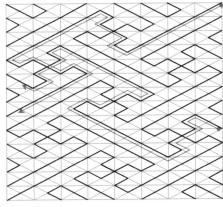

Mark a grid – the sample a is ½ x 1in diagonal grid. Use the *sayagata* stitch sequence described opposite. The stitching lines are now on the diagonal.

Sayagata kuzushi
(cursive sayagata)

This makes a good border pattern. Like *amimon* (page 70), it is similar to patterns traditionally stitched by the Ainu people of Hokkaido (see page 13).

 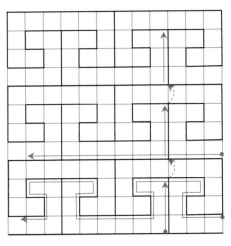

Mark a grid – the sample is ½in. Following the red arrows, stitch horizontal lines (red), keeping thread continuous and stranding across the back, indicated in the diagram by red dashed lines. Stitch around the stepped pattern (brown) and finish by stitching the vertical lines (yellow).

Kūji kuzushi
(simple I-form)

This is made from a repeat of the kanji character *ku* or *kou* (artisan, manufacture or work), shown below. *Kuzushiji* refers to the simplest forms of kanji characters. Using this pattern for work clothes would be a visual pun!

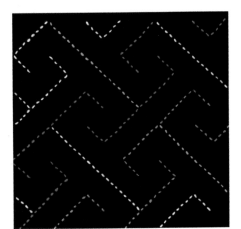 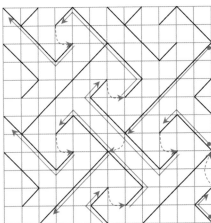

Mark a grid – the sample is ½in. Use the grid to mark diagonal pattern lines. Following the red arrows, stitch the pattern in diagonal sections (red and light brown), keeping thread continuous and stranding across the back. Finish by stitching the straight diagonal lines (yellow), keeping thread continuous as before.

MOTIFS

Sashiko is often accented with motifs, against plain backgrounds or an all-over sashiko pattern. Make cardboard templates for simple motifs and transfer more complex designs using the chaco paper or dressmaker's carbon method described on page 22. This selection is intended only as a starting point – you will find many more motifs you can adapt for stitching by looking at more general books about Japanese textile design (see Bibliography on page 125).

Stitching sashiko within another shape is another design option. This is more difficult than stitching within a square or rectangle. If the pattern grid fits with the shape, such as *sayagata*, *higaki* or *kagome* stitched within *matsukawabishi* motifs (see the *noren* curtain on page 44) it is relatively easy. Working within a complicated shape, such as the large panel '*Noshi*' (page 7) is much harder, as there is no straight edge to the pattern.

Single pattern repeats within a square are an easier way to begin. These appear on many very old sashiko coats and waistcoats, usually set within another pattern, such as squares set within the stepped version of *yamagata* (page 74) or on simple stripes. A modern version of this arrangement covers the back of the coat on page 120. See the selection of single motifs from Shōnai (below left); each could be developed into an all-over repeat design.

Flowers and leaves

These can give your work a seasonal theme. Some motifs are strongly associated with certain seasons, such as *sakura* (cherry blossom) in spring. As a rough guide, choose what is in flower for the season you wish to depict or refer to books about Japanese design for ideas. Be aware that some flowering seasons are very short. Japanese style anticipates the change in seasons – it would just not be *iki* (chic) to wear one's red *momiji* (maple leaf) kimono when the leaves have actually begun to turn!

ume (plum)

sakura (cherry)

take (bamboo)

momiji (maple)

kiku (chrysanthemum)

kikyō (bellflower)

left: A selection of motifs for single use or as all-over repeat designs.

Kamon
(family crests)

These were used by nobles from the Heian era (794–1185), by warriors during the Kamakura era (1185–1392) and by commoners since the Edo era (1615–1868). All kinds of designs are used but most *mon* (crests) are circular. Women inherit their mother's *mon* while men inherit their father's. *Kamon* are still used on formal kimono, *furoshiki* (wrapping cloth – see page 14) or *fukusa* (a square cloth to cover gifts of money). For an example of *mon* used to decorate a *noren* curtain, see page 121. If you would like to use *mon*, select a design that appeals to you – there are thousands of them. If it is solid black on white, the most formal version of *mon* that appears in most pattern books, you will need to make an outline drawing. *Marumon* are circular motifs similar to crests but not legally recognized as such. They are considered unique to Japanese design.

Detail of modern *furoshiki* wrapping cloth, with *kamon* (family crest), bamboo and snowflake design.

moon and cloud

paulownia

maple leaf circle

triple wisteria

double rice sheaf

iris

seigaiha coin

temple gong

Kanji
(Chinese characters)

These are one of three systems used together to write Japanese. Combining kanji with other design elements began among the aristocracy during the Kamakura era (1185–1392). It is called *ashide* (reed calligraphy) and would adapt beautifully to sashiko. Selected kanji from Chinese poems were arranged within pictorial designs to reflect the poem. Kanji are more traditionally used in sashiko to stitch the owner's name on *furoshiki*, very useful when they are used to wrap gifts and should be returned to the sender with another gift inside! You can enlarge and use these kanji or research others for your sashiko.

春	夏	秋	冬	安
spring	summer	fall/autumn	winter	peaceful
子	父	母	友	会
child	father	mother	friend	club/group
学	里	森	海	雪
learning	village	forest	ocean	snow
地	糸	色	花	美
earth	thread	colour	flower	beauty

Design Traditions

'Traditional' Japanese design, with its emphasis on asymmetry, dates from the early Edo era (1615–1868) and introduced everyday items (books, calligraphy, tea ceremony items, bridges, chess pieces and so on) as design elements. Late Edo era sumptuary laws severely curbed the outward show of wealth in dress, fuelling a new fashion for understated chic or *iki*, epitomized by dark stripes, *kasuri* ikat and *edo komon* ('small pattern' fabric stencilled in Tokyo), patterns which appeared almost immediately in sashiko. Many motif combinations were established, such as *shō chiku bai* (pine, plum and bamboo – the 'three friends of winter'). A subtle interpretation could be plum blossoms and bamboo leaves against a *matsukawabishi* background (page 84) or pine boughs and plum blossoms against *kagome* (page 83). Bamboo on its own represents strength and endurance. *Matsu* (pine) is a homonym for 'wait' so it is regarded as the dwelling place of the gods. It is part of the New Year *kadomatsu* (pine gate) decorations, and is placed in pairs outside the front door.

AUSPICIOUS MOTIFS

These make interesting accents. Some large modern sashiko pieces are adapted from old *tsutsugaki* (rice paste resist) textiles, which are now very rare but once dominated bridal trousseaus. The effect of white sashiko stitches on indigo is similar to the undyed lines left by the resist paste. These were large textiles including *yogi* (kimono-shaped quilt, page 10), *futon* (fold-up mattress), *yutan* (cloth for covering furniture) and *furoshiki* (wrapping cloth). Designs usually included the bride's *kamon* (family crest).

Noshi

This was originally a bundle of dried strips of abalone used to decorate ritual offerings. This edible shellfish was considered to be the food of the gods. It is usually depicted like a bundle of ribbons or fabric strips and is one of the most impressive motifs for kimono. *Noshi* also decorate special gifts. The word is a homonym for 'extend', so it symbolizes longevity. See page 121 for an example of *noshi* in sashiko.

Tsurukame
(crane and tortoise)

These motifs symbolize longevity. Bridal textiles often show them together or paired. The tortoise is often represented just by its hexagonal shell pattern (as shown by the stitched patterns below). *Orizuru* (origami cranes) are a popular motif and adapt well to sashiko. Other birds and animals include the tiger (bravery) and a pair of mandarin ducks (a well-matched couple).

crane and pine needles

Ogi
(folding fan)

This auspicious motif represents increase. A multitude of fan papers would make a good layout for a sashiko sampler.

five fans

folding fan

Takarazukushi
(treasure collection)

A treasure collection includes a gold ingot (shaped like *fundō*, page 65), a flaming wish-granting jewel, lucky mallet, storehouse key, cloak of invisibility, rush hat, magic clove, treasure bag and other items which vary from region to region in Japan. You could, of course, add some of your own!

treasure bag

wish-granting jewel

treasure key

hat

Hōō
(phoenix)

The phoenix is said to appear during a reign of peace and happiness. As the magical bird will only alight on a paulownia tree, the two motifs usually appear together.

HITOMEZASHI SASHIKO PATTERNS

Hitomezashi (one stitch sashiko) designs are worked as a grid of straight lines, where stitches meet or cross to make the design. Most names end with *zashi* (a mutation from sashi), which translates best as 'stitch', but all the stitches are really running stitch. Some patterns have vertical and horizontal rows, others have additional diagonal lines while some have horizontal stitches only.

The patterns start with the easiest, with significant parts of the pattern stitched in different colours. The grid dictates the stitch size. For all *hitomezashi*, stitch along the first row, turn your work and stitch back along the next row – first horizontally, then vertically, then diagonally, as required by the pattern. Additional instructions and information are given with the designs.

The diagrams show the grids in blue, stitching lines in black, stitching direction in red arrows with a red dot to show the starting point. Red dashed lines indicate where thread should be stranded loosely across the back of the work. Some patterns have shaded backgrounds to show you where to begin stitching and some patterns with more elaborate grids have a separate grid diagram in blue.

The first 30 patterns, up to *jizashi* (ground stitch, page 104), are stitched on a ¼in (6mm) or ³⁄₁₆in (5mm) square grid, except *ajirozashi* (threaded stitch, page 103). Use the smaller grid only with fine sashiko thread. Suitable grid dimensions for all other designs are given with each pattern. See also page 20 for drawing patterns using grids.

HITOMEZASHI STITCHING TIPS

- Start and finish *hitomezashi* with a simple quilter's knot.
- Use the *hatamusubi* joining knot to keep thread continuous (see page 24).
- To mark square grids quickly, see page 22.
- Many *hitomezashi* patterns have a long, stranded threads on the back which are visible on finished items, so you may want to use these for lined projects.
- Like all dense stitching, *hitomezashi* will pull in your work more than *moyōzashi* patterns, so leave a loop for ease when turning at the end of each row (see below), indicated by red dashed lines in diagrams.

Grid Measurements

The grids for the following *hitomezashi* patterns are based on imperial measurements but are easy to convert to metric using the following formula:

> To convert inches to centimetres,
> multiply the measurement in inches by 2.54,
> e.g., 2in × 2.54 = 5.08cm

See page 20 for the commonly used imperial-metric conversions in this book.

Yokogushi
(horizontal rows)

This basic stitch forms the first step of many other patterns: old sashiko used it a lot. Stitch back and forth across the grid. The position of the stitches and gaps alternates between one row and the next. Accurate base rows are important – the stitches should go exactly across one grid square, on the horizontal line. *Yokogushi* may be turned through 90 degrees to become vertical lines, when it forms the basis of other patterns.

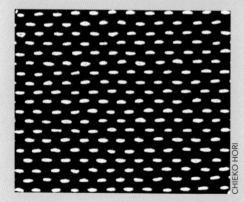

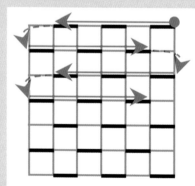

CHIEKO HORI

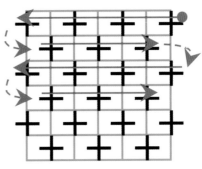

Jūjizashi
('10' cross stitch)

This begins as *yokogushi* (opposite). The second set of stitches cross over the first at right angles. Note there is no grid line to guide these – just line them up by eye. This is one of the *hitomezashi* patterns where the stitches cross, creating a raised texture. It is the basis for *komezashi* (rice stitch, below), *komezashi* variations and *kusari jujizashi* (chain cross stitch, overleaf).

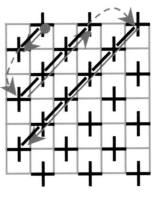

Komezashi
(rice stitch)

This looks like the kanji character for rice (see below). It was stitched with hopes for a good harvest and is a very dense stitch. Begin with *jūjizashi* (above) and stitch extra diagonal lines, taking a small stitch behind each cross. Work all diagonal stitches leaning in one direction and then complete the other diagonal. It is a hardwearing stitch, good for bags (see red bag on page 49).

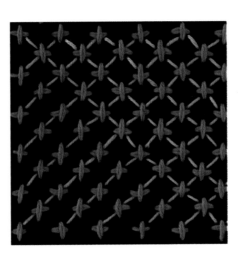

Kawari komezashi
(rice stitch variation)

In this version, the diagonal stitches are between the crosses, rather than linking the cross centres. This variation was used for many *donza* fishermen's coats from Awaji Island. See overleaf for more *komezashi* variations.

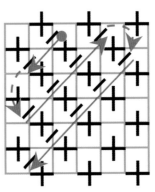

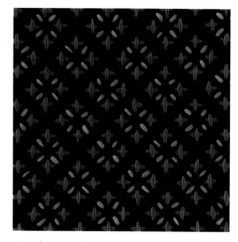

For another *komezashi* variation, try leaving the alternate diagonal rows unstitched.

Work each zigzag line in this variation separately, changing direction and making zigzags as large as you wish.

Stitching only alternate diagonal rows between the crosses gives the illusion of tiny squares on point.

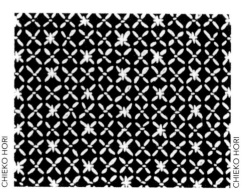

Enlarging the basic grid size opens up further possibilities with this pretty flower motif. At the point where the horizontal and diagonal lines would cross, take two stitches rather than one, with a consistent gap in between. Stitch the diagonal lines the same way, with an extra stitch in between the 'flowers' (see the denim tote bag on page 40).

Try these ideas for varying the basic *jūjizashi* and *komezashi* patterns – stitching flower crosses with thicker 'petals' (two parallel rows of running stitch), and stitching flower crosses with diagonal rows forming smaller crosses and diagonal lines on a ground where only alternate horizontal rows are crossed vertically.

Kusari jūjizashi
(chain cross stitch)

This is also known as *jūjizashi tsunagi* (linked cross stitch) and *masuzashi* (square measure stitch) – it is not uncommon for one stitch to have several names in different regions. Diagonal stitches link the points of the crosses. The pattern begins with *jūjizashi* (page 97) as the base.

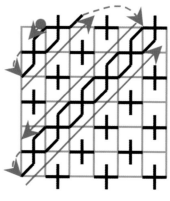

Dan tsunagi
(linked steps)

This is a miniature version of the larger pattern on page 74. Starting with *yokogushi* (page 96) as the base, the ends of horizontal and vertical stitches meet to make the pattern. The ends of meeting stitches do not have to go through exactly the same hole in the fabric but should look as if they are meeting neatly, while keeping the rows straight. *Takenohanezashi* (hawk's feather stitch) is based on *dan tsunagi* with extra diagonal lines in one direction only, shown lower left in the coloured stitch sample.

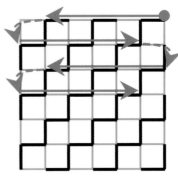

Zenizashi
(coin stitch)

This is based on a grid of little squares. It was stitched for prosperity and looks like a Japanese coin, with a hole in the middle. The first row of *yokogushi* (page 96) is repeated and, in every row, the stitches and gaps are in the same place. Alternate diagonal lines are stitched afterwards, in two stages. Some people overlap the diagonal stitches into the squares, while others meet at the corners or leave a little gap. It is all a matter of personal sashiko style! When every diagonal line is stitched (right), the pattern is called *honzenizashi* (real coin stitch).

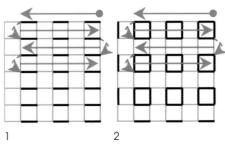

1   2

Komenohanazashi
(rice flower stitch)

This pattern is stitched on the same square grid but the stitches are aligned differently. First work the horizontal rows with the stitches between the vertical lines. The vertical rows are stitched the same way and then diagonal lines in two directions complete the pattern.

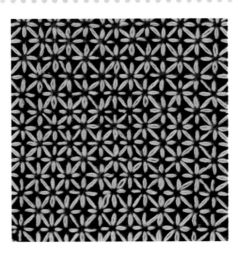

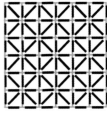

1   2

Hanashijūshi
(flower cross)

This pattern includes shorter stitches in the horizontal rows. Stitch the vertical rows first, on the vertical lines but between the horizontal lines (shown as red lines on the diagram), like the stitch rows for *komenohanazashi*, previously.

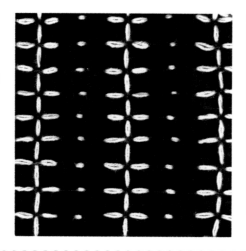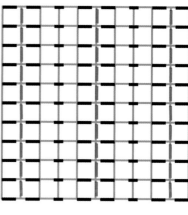

Kagome
(woven bamboo)

This is the *hitomezashi* version of the *moyōzashi* pattern (see *kagome*, page 83). It follows the same stitch sequence as the larger design but with one stitch only in each diagonal section. Stitch the vertical lines first, as for *komenohanazashi* (page 99), then complete the pattern in one diagonal direction, then the other.

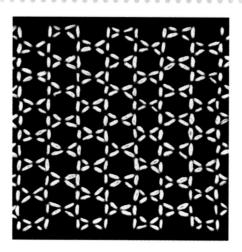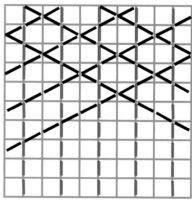

Kakinohanazashi
(persimmon flower stitch)

This appears in many regions and is also known as *hanazashi* (flower stitch). The fruits are an autumn treat. This design combines alternate rows, like *yokogushi* (page 96) with pairs that are the same, like the *zenizashi* base rows (page 99). Stitch back and forth across the grid, as shown in the diagram by the black and red rows. Pattern rows shown in red are repeats of the previous row. If the rows are not aligned according to the correct sequence, they will not interlock properly and the pattern won't appear. Note, the rows have one stitch followed by one gap, with no double gaps.

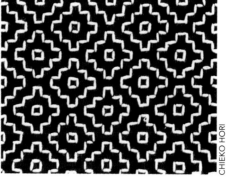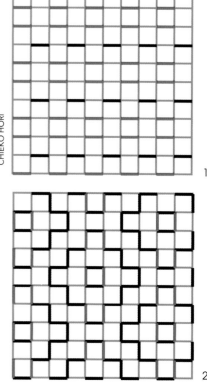

CHIEKO HORI

1

2

Jūjizashi
('10' cross stitch)

This has the same name as the pattern on page 97 but has larger crosses. It uses the same first step as *kakinohanazashi* (opposite) and then the vertical rows are stitched in identical pairs. Alternate between bands of *kakinohanazashi* and *jūjizashi* by changing the second step sequence of pairs and single rows (see the beige sampler cushion on page 39). You will discover some more variations of these by accident if you lose count!

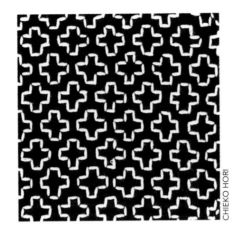 

Yamagata
(mountain form)

This can also use the same first step as *kakinohanazashi* or *sanjū kakinohanazashi* (below). The first version is shown in the diagram and the second in the stitched sample. The first step becomes the vertical rows, while the diagonal rows are stitched following the instructions for *yokogushi* (page 96).

 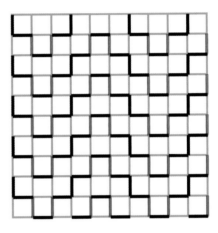

Stitching the first step like *yokogushi* but pairing the two rows in the centre creates a variation of *kakinohanazashi* and *yamagata*. These patterns suggest infinite increase. To centre these patterns within a square, stitch the two centre lines first and work outwards.

Sanjū kakinohanazashi
(triple persimmon flower stitch)

This is also called *nijū kakinohanazashi* (double persimmon flower stitch). Whatever the name, the effect of one flower inside another requires more alternate rows in step one than the single flower. There are four alternate rows between each matching pair. In step two, there are only three alternate rows.

 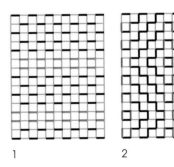

1   2

Igetazashi
(well curb stitch)

This is tricky as there are double and triple gaps between the stitches as well as single gaps. There is also a repeated pair of rows in both the first and second step. To help you follow this pattern, the *igeta* shapes have been shaded in the diagrams. Like the *kakinohanazashi* and *yamagata* variations previously, work the pattern from the centre two rows outwards to line it up within a square. The pattern imitates expensive *kasuri* ikat cotton, once very fashionable.

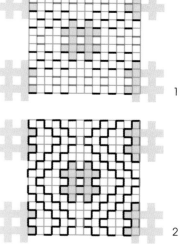

AYAME ENDO

1

2

Jijūhishikaha
(woven cross diamond)

This is the easiest of several threaded stitches. The cross base is stitched following the instructions for *komezashi* (page 97) but with some horizontal lines left uncrossed by stitching alternate vertical lines only. See page 82 for more information about the significance of diamond patterns. Follow the red zigzag lines for the threading sequence. Start and finish the threaded sections at the red dots with a simple knot on the wrong side. On a small sample, strand across the back from one row to the next, making sure you have enough thread to go right across the row.

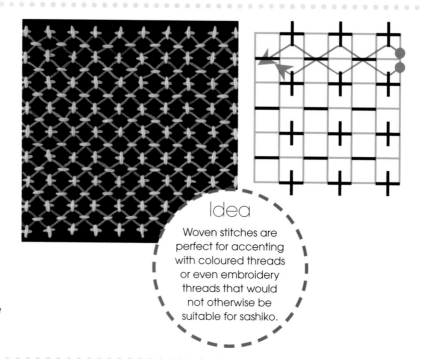

Idea

Woven stitches are perfect for accenting with coloured threads or even embroidery threads that would not otherwise be suitable for sashiko.

Kawari kikkōzashi
(tortoiseshell stitch variation)

This is a threaded version of *yokogushi* (page 96) but with the foundation stitched as vertical, not horizontal, lines. See page 86 for more information about hexagonal patterns. Follow the red zigzag lines for the threading sequence, as above. For the variation, stitch horizontal rows of running stitch inside the hexagons, shown in turquoise in the stitched sample (see greetings cards on page 28).

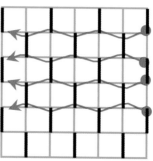

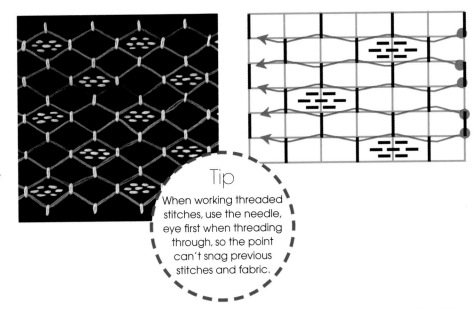

Ajirozashi
(threaded stitch)

This begins as a slightly larger version of *kawari kikkōzashi*. Use a ¼ x ⅜in grid so the gap between the running stitches is wider. Fill in alternate hexagons in every other row with three rows of running stitch, traditionally worked from side to side, stranding across the back of the work between stitches.

Tip

When working threaded stitches, use the needle, eye first when threading through, so the point can't snag previous stitches and fabric.

Ishidatami
(paving block)

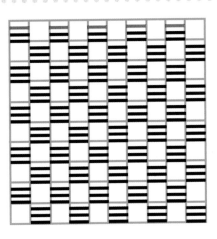

CHIEKO HORI

This is also known as *arare* (hailstone) and *ichimatsuzashi* (*Ichimatsu* stitch) after Kabuki actor Sanogawa Ichimatsu I (1722–62), who adopted the pattern as a pun on his name – *ichimatsu* means 'one square'. Three stitches form the basic unit, stitched by stacking up rows of single running stitches, repeated alternately. The red stitches on the diagram indicate the start of the pattern and the part to be repeated. Take care that your stitches are exactly aligned. If using fine sashiko thread, you may need to stitch four rows in each unit, as shown in the stitched sample.

Kasuri koshi
(kasuri check)

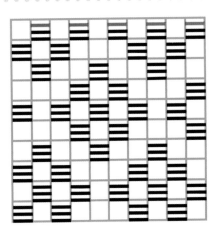

CHIEKO HORI

This copies a simple pattern used for Kurume *kasuri* ikat, woven in Kyushu. Kurume *kasuri* has been popular since it was invented in the late 18th century and large stylized geometric patterns were used for bedding. Like *ishidatami* (above), the pattern is stitched from side to side with three or four stitches one above the other in each square. The red stitches in the diagram indicate the pattern repeat.

Masugata
(square form)

This uses the same square unit as *ishidatami* and *kasuri koshi*. *Masuzashi*, the *moyōzashi* pattern on page 61 is also named after the traditional square wooden measuring box. Stitch the pattern the same way as the two previous designs.

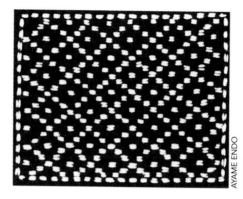

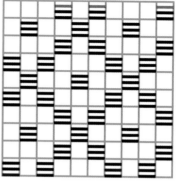

AYAME ENDO

Jizashi
(ground stitch)

This and the variation below can be easily adapted for border designs. The narrow line is two immediately adjacent rows of running stitch, with the gap about half the length of the stitch (like the *moyōzashi* running stitch), with one row offset. It is often used on its own to separate different areas of sashiko within a larger design or as an outline. To help you read the diagram, the first pattern section has a shaded background. Stitch rows back and forth horizontally. Take care to line up the stitches forming the double columns and offset the stitches to create the other motifs.

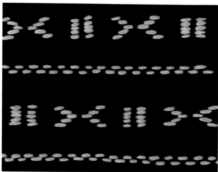

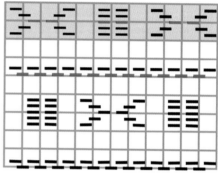

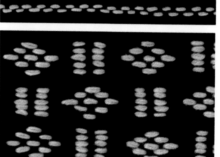

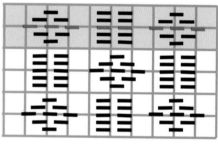

Urokozashi
(fish scale stitch)

This pattern was stitched in hopes of a good catch. The pattern is also associated with serpents, both in *Nōh* drama and story of Hojo Tokimasa in the Kamakura era (1185–1392). He prayed he would be able to end civil war. A sea serpent appeared, turned into a beautiful woman and granted his wish but left three scales behind. To work this pattern, first mark a ½ x ⅜in grid. To help you read the diagram, the first pattern section has a shaded background. Stitch rows back and forth consecutively and begin each pattern section with the row shown in red.

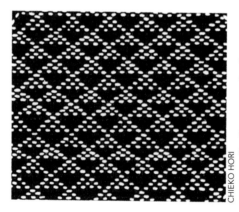

CHIEKO HORI

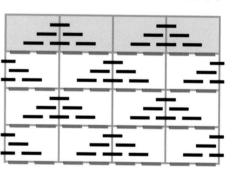

Hishizashi
(diamond stitch)

This pattern is associated with increase (for more information see Diamonds, page 82). Mark a 1 x ⅝in grid. Start stitching along the row shown in red on the shaded background. Stitch the second and third rows on either side of the first. Stitch the fourth and fifth on either side again, building up the diamond shape. Begin the next section with the centre row shown in red. For a variation, leave out the small stitches between individual diamonds.

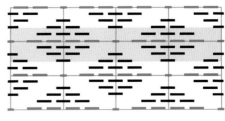

CHIEKO HORI

Hanabishizashi
(flower diamond stitch)

This uses the same diamond motif sewn in intersecting diagonal lines. Mark a 1½in square grid and add diagonal lines. Stitch the first row of each section along the diagonal line, shown in red on the shaded background, and build up the pattern on either side of this row, as for *hishizashi* (above). On a slightly larger grid, increase the number of stitches in the first row and add extra rows on the outside of the 'petals'.

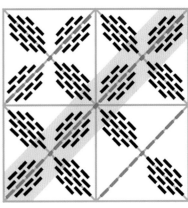

CHIEKO HORI

Hishitsunagi
(linked diamond)

This looks difficult but begins with rows of diamonds like *hishizashi* (above). Mark a grid with vertical lines 1in apart. Each diamond section has seven horizontal lines ½in apart and is ⅞in from the next section. The distance between the diamond sections can be altered to make the pattern fit a given area. Stitch each diamond row the same way as *hishizashi*, then stitch the linking diagonals in consecutive rows to the top of the next diamond. It is easier to stitch all the diamond sections first and then link them.

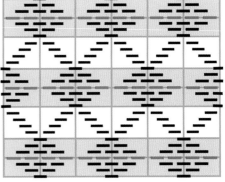

CHIEKO HORI

Nagarebishi
(flowing diamond)

This pattern separates the diamonds visually with a zigzag line, although they are stitched as part of the same rows. Mark a 1 x $\frac{7}{8}$in grid and add diagonal zigzag lines, not quite connecting the horizontal lines. Stitch each diamond row the same way as *hishizashi* (page 105), but with seven rows completing each pattern section.

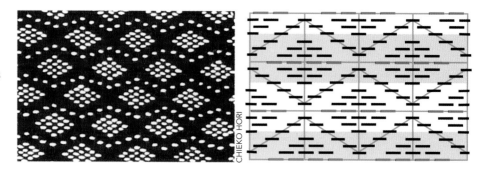

CHIEKO HORI

Kawaribishi
(diamond variation)

This forms a diagonal grid with little diamonds in the centre. Mark a grid $\frac{3}{4}$ x $\frac{1}{2}$in, then mark diagonal lines. Stitch each row the same way as *hishizashi* (page 105), but with only four rows completing the pattern. To fit the pattern easily to a square outline, begin with a $\frac{1}{2}$in grid.

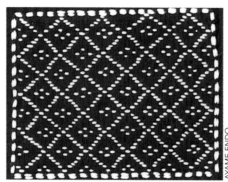

AYAME ENDO

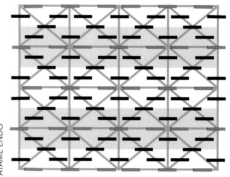

Takedabishi
(Takeda diamond)

This is a well-known family crest of four connected diamonds. Mark a 1½ x 1in grid, mark diagonal lines and mark extra diagonals to define the diamonds, as shown in the separate blue grid diagram below. Start stitching along the row shown in red on the shaded background. Stitch the blue line above, returning to fill in the two black rows in between, then repeat for the green row and finish the first section. This is a traditional way to break down this design for stitching. The stitched sample shows a variation – follow the pattern but leave out the infill stitches for all the diamonds.

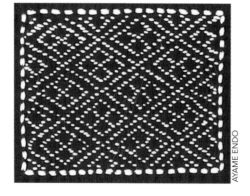

AYAME ENDO

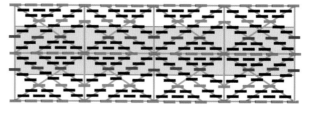

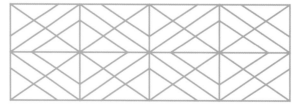

Kasuri tsunagi
(linked kasuri)

This is another pattern inspired by popular textile designs of the Edo era (1615–1868). The number of stitches in the diagonal links can vary or be left out altogether for an unlinked pattern. The motifs resemble little flowers. Mark a ½in grid. For each section, start stitching along the row shown in red on the shaded background, then stitch the three rows above. Stitch the two rows below the red row and then the link stitches.

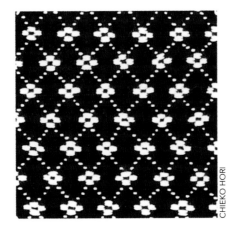

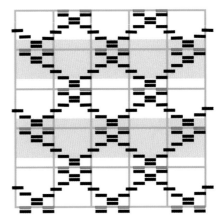

CHIEKO HORI

Hanakikkō
(flower tortoiseshell)

This is an example of a filled hexagon design. Mark a ½ x ¼in grid. Stitch each hexagon row the same way as *kasuri tsunagi* (above), then stitch the link diagonals in consecutive rows to the top of the next hexagon. The variation replaces the centre 'flower' with three parallel running stitches.

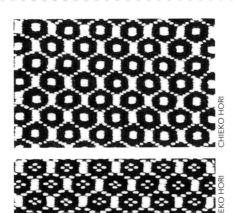

CHIEKO HORI

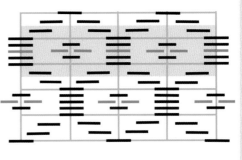

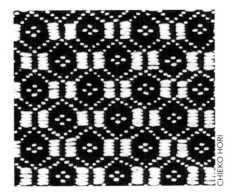

CHIEKO HORI

Futometsunagi
(linked bold stitch)

This is based on a tortoiseshell hexagon. Mark a ⅜ x ¼in grid and add diagonal lines, as shown in the separate blue grid diagram. Stitch each hexagon centre row the same way as *jizashi* variation on page 104, then stitch the link diagonals in consecutive rows to the top of the next hexagon. Note the stitch length varies between the bold blocks, 'flower' centres and link diagonals.

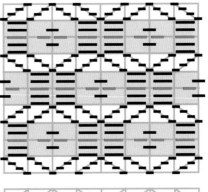

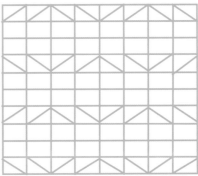

CHIEKO HORI

Gazashi
(moth stitch)

This is traditional to Yuza-machi, Shōnai. Mark vertical lines at ⅝in and ½in intervals alternately and horizontal lines at ⅝in. Following the diagram begin each row of moths with the long stitches (marked in red), decreasing the stitch length towards the end of the body. Stitch the antennae last – their exact shape and size is a matter of personal taste! *Gazashi* can be stitched individually as a scattered pattern.

AYAME ENDO

Mukaichiyōzashi
(facing butterfly)

This is a very old stitch used for the shoulder panel and strap of *sorihikihappi* (sled-hauling waistcoat) – see page 13. Like the following two stitches, the stitch is identical on the back. Mark vertical lines at 1¼in and ¼in intervals alternately and horizontal lines at ⅝in intervals. Stitch each row of butterflies in the same way as *gazashi* (above).

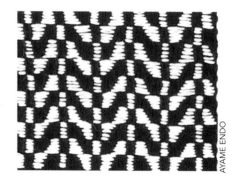

AYAME ENDO

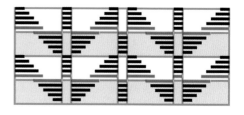

Sugizashi
(cedar stitch)

This pattern looks like wood grain. Fragrant cedar wood is used in traditional buildings in Japan and also to keep moths away from stored clothing. Mark a ¼in grid and diagonal lines. Stitch the lines shown in red in sequence and then fill in the lines in between.

CHIEKO HORI

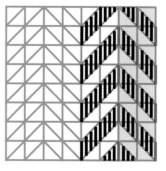

Idea

All of the stitches on these two pages would be ideal to adapt for counted embroidery.

Yabanezashi
(arrow stitch)

This is sewn on the same grid and in the same sequence as the previous pattern *sugizashi*. Note the break in the design at the points. Like other arrow patterns, it is linked to the samurai warrior tradition (for more information see *yabane*, page 75).

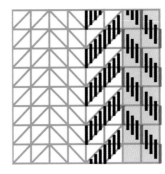

CHIEKO HORI

Sorobanzashi
(abacus stitch)

This is another stitch traditional to Yuza-machi, Shōnai. Because it resembles abacus beads, it represents prosperity. It is one of the most difficult stitches to do well. Mark a ½in grid. Stitch each diamond row the same way as *hishizashi* (page 105), but with seven rows completing each pattern section. Concentrate on keeping the abacus 'rods' straight!

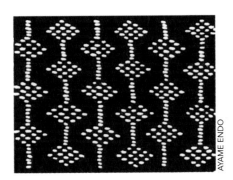

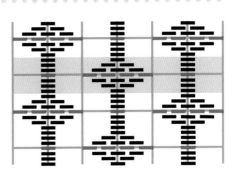

AYAME ENDO

Nanamezashi
(slanting stitch)

This stitch can slant in either direction. Mark a ¼in grid and add diagonal lines, as shown in the separate blue grid diagram. Stitch the red lines first and the other two black lines in each 'step' group in sequence before moving on to the next. The shaded background shows one pattern repeat. Maintaining the illusion of straight diagonal lines made from stepped stitches is difficult yet the finished sashiko has a simple elegance.

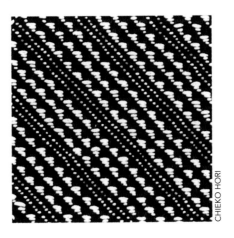

CHIEKO HORI

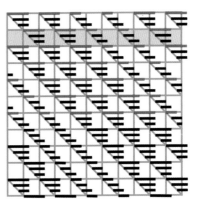

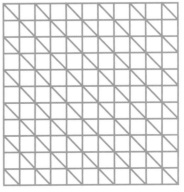

INSPIRATION GALLERY

If you have been practising your sashiko and have mastered a selection of patterns, you might be looking for something bigger to really test your sashiko skills! No doubt you will want to take sashiko in your own direction, so this section shows various modern samplers, quilts and wearable artworks to fire up your imagination. There are examples of sashiko combined with patchwork and quilting, on patterned fabric, with coloured thread, in elaborate outlines and combinations, as well as traditional samplers and sashiko stitched as embroidery.

Today, the focus has shifted from practical necessity to an interest in sashiko's decorative possibilities. Sashiko may be worked through quilt wadding (batting), stitched as embroidery or included in patchwork, often with fabrics printed with Japanese designs. It has become high fashion, decorating modern clothing and household goods.

We are lucky that older women who learned sashiko from their grandmother's generation handed on their legacy just in time, such as Tetsue Ikeda, who, in her late 70s, began a sashiko class in Yuza-machi, Yamagata Prefecture. She had learned sashiko as a child, from her grandmother's generation. Some of the works featured on the following pages are by her former students or stitchers who learned sashiko from Yoshimi Arakawa, who was also taught by Tetsue. Similar stories of sashiko's survival and revival can be found in other regions of Japan.

My friends and sashiko teachers have kindly allowed me to include photographs of their work in this gallery. All of the pieces were exhibited as part of the 'Magic of Sashiko' exhibition at the inaugural Festival of Quilts in Birmingham, England, 2003.

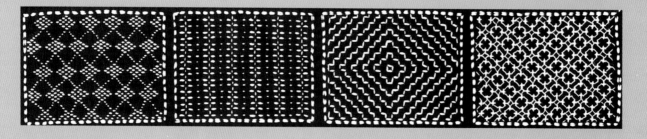

Yuza Sashiko Sampler
contemporary work by Ayame Endo

Forty-two different *hitomezashi* patterns traditionally stitched in Yuza-machi are shown on this sampler, in white thread on indigo. The border has a design of individual *kakinohanazashi* flowers (page 100) with pairs of flower petals from the *hanabishizashi* design (page 105). This large sampler is a valuable record of Yuza sashiko patterns from the second half of the 20th century. It was specially created for the 'Magic of Sashiko' exhibition.

Table Centre Samplers
**contemporary works by Chitako Sato (left)
and Chie Ikeda (below)**

Samplers are a way of handing down stitches in Yuza-machi, where Tetsue Ikeda began teaching traditional sashiko in the late 1970s. Both samplers show the basic stitches of Yuza sashiko – mainly *hitomezashi* patterns, arranged with a central medallion based on *asanoha* (page 72), with border stitches and corner designs included. Traditional indigo cloth is used, just 14½in wide, and the samplers are stitched through one layer only.

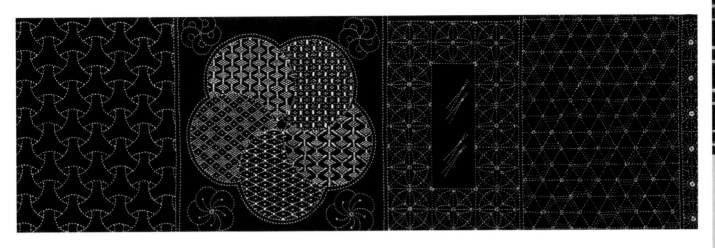

Shonai Sashiko Sampler
contemporary work by Chieko Hori

Dozens of patterns cover this long roll of black cotton from end to end, showing examples of every sashiko technique, including designs from Shōnai, Yuza-machi, Honjyo-shi and Tobishima. A whole *tan* (fabric roll) is 13 yards long and 14½in wide and is the exact amount of fabric required for one kimono. Chieko has also shown many different ways of laying out patterns, such as the *matsukawabishi* sampler on a background of *seigaiha* (page 68) and *hishi seigaiha* (page 83), and the arrangement of various small patterns within a large plum blossom outline. The rectangular border with scattered pine needle motifs at its centre shows a complex variation on the basic *shippō* pattern (page 64), with individual pattern repeats similar to the old Shōnai square designs on page 92. Variations on the *yamagata* design (based on *dan tsunagi*, page 74) and other large patterns are complemented by numerous large hexagons filled in with *hitomezashi* designs, arranged according to stitch group.

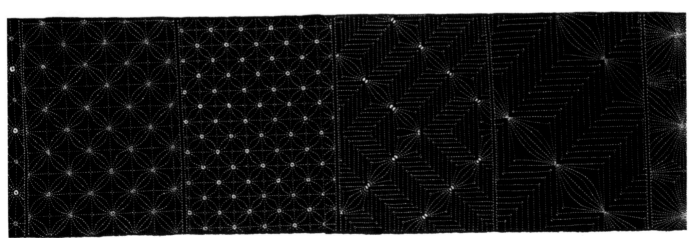

Uwatsupari
woman's outer coat
by Eiko Sasaki, 1975

Various sashiko patterns are
very skillfully arranged on
this narrow-sleeved coat. The
individual pattern shapes
of *hishizashi* (page 105) and
kakinohanazashi (page 100) are
harmoniously used to create
the edges of the stitched
areas on the shoulders and
lower body. The flared collar
is stitched all over with *kawari
sayagata* (page 91), also called
rinzu, after the damask kimono
silk frequently woven in this
pattern. Cross-over jackets and
coats, with integral fabric ties,
are traditional country women's
wear in Japan.

Chabaori
woman's short jacket by Kiyoko Shibuya, 1970

Using shaded or variegated thread is an interesting way of breaking up a pattern to give visual interest and resemble *kasuri* ikat. Here *asanoha* (page 72) is stitched all over in variegated indigo thread on indigo fabric. The thread shades from white to the same indigo as the cloth, so the hemp leaves subtly merge into the background. When stitching *asanoha*, women hoped that the person wearing the sashiko would enjoy good health. It was a popular pattern for babies' clothes.

Waistcoat

by Kiyoko Saito, 1980

Kiyoko recycled the fabric from a skirt she wore as a student to make this traditional *sodenashi* waistcoat. She enjoyed the brilliance of the coloured threads, carefully planned to enhance the patterns that include *bishamon kikkō* (page 88), *kakinohanazashi* (page 100), a variation on *ajiro* (page 77) and a border design on the collar, adapted from *hishizashi* (page 105). The large *manji* symbol on the back is filled in with various *hitomezashi* stitches (see circular detail above).

Mukenishyoi
**crested ceremonial waistcoat
by Eiko Sasaki, 1973**

These waistcoats are traditionally worn at weddings in
Yuza by the bridegroom's attendants, who go ahead and
announce to the neighbours that the groom is coming
to collect his bride. The *kamon* crest is therefore that of
the bridegroom, whereas the bride's trousseau will be
decorated with her own crest, inherited from her mother
(see *kamon*, page 93). The *mukenishyoi* is the same
basic shape as the *sodenashi*, worn for everyday, but
the addition of the crest gives a garment much higher
formal status, suitable for a special occasion. *Sanju
kakinohanazashi* (page 101) is stitched in ochre thread as
a band right round the waistcoat, with the collar cover
decorated with *kusari jūjizashi* (page 98). The rest of the
waistcoat is stitched with diagonal parallel lines forming
huge *yamagata* or mountain shapes in blue.

Waistcoat
contemporary work by Chie Ikeda

This waistcoat has a variety of patterns worked in bands using hand-dyed threads sent from the United Kingdom, each outlined with a double running stitch line (see *jizashi* page 104). The brilliant colours of some of the threads are toned down by the charcoal grey fabric. As most of the threads were the equivalent of thick sashiko thread, Chie has experimented with using a single thread for patterns that traditionally use double thread.

Sashiko and Patchwork Quilt
contemporary work by Chie Ikeda, with design input from Reiko Domon

This was Chie's combination of sashiko and patchwork in a large piece. It is a record of sashiko patterns stitched in Yuza-machi. The sashiko was stitched as embroidery before piecing and quilting in the ditch along the seam lines, where she carefully matched her thread to the fabric. It was wadded (batted) with polyester. Restrained use of indigo and white shows off the sashiko patterns clearly. The threads are white and very pale ice blue, the colour of old sashiko where indigo has migrated from fabric to thread.

Coat
**contemporary work by
Chie Ikeda**

Various Shonai sashiko stitches
adorn the back of this coat in
a modern interpretation of a
traditional pattern arrangement.
Like old sashiko jackets, Chie
has used a very dense stitch
sorobanzashi (page 109) on the
shoulders and also used sashiko
to reinforce the pockets. After
the sashiko was complete, the
coat was professionally tailored.

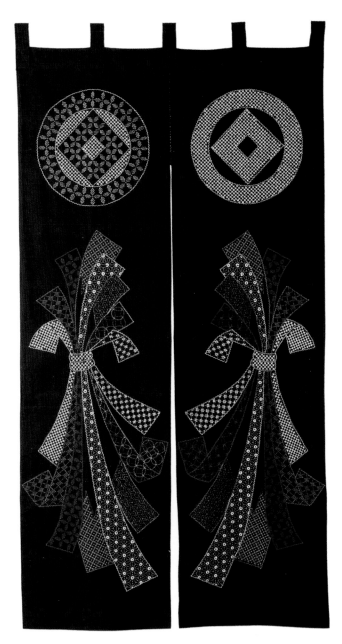

Front of curtain

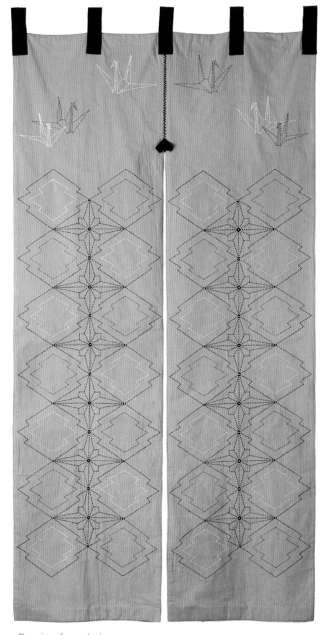

Back of curtain

Noren door curtain
contemporary work by Chieko Hori

Chieko combined the Hori family *kamon* (family crest) and twin *noshi* motifs (page 94) with fillings of various sashiko stitches in coloured thread on indigo fabric for this *noren* curtain. Stitching within a variable outline is difficult as there is no straight line at the pattern edge. The stitches follow the movement of the individual *noshi* strips. The crest is filled in with *komezashi* (page 97) on the right, reversed to make a negative image on the left, with the circle and square accented with *hanabishizashi* (page 105), adapted to follow the curve. As *noren* are seen from both sides, the back is decorated with a variation of *matsukawabishi* (page 84) with distorted *yatsude asanoha* (page 67) in the central motif. *Orizuru* (origami cranes, page 94) decorate the top. Each panel uses the full width of traditional cloth, approximately 14½in wide, and all the sashiko was completed before the panels were sewn together. For construction details, see the *noren* curtain on page 44.

Denshō (Tradition)
patchwork quilt by Reiko Domon, 2002

This quilt, which combines Shōnai sashiko with patchwork and quilting, was awarded the Olympus Thread Company Prize at Quilt Week, Yokohama 2002. Reiko wanted to picture a local legend, which says that winter comes to Yuza-machi when a flock of swans bringing snow is seen flying over Mount Chōkai. The abundant spring melt water fills the rice fields, so the snow is the source of the area's prosperity. The sashiko represents the snow and the river. Reiko says that one of the pleasures of quilting in winter is sitting around the *kotatsu* (a low table with a heater underneath, which has replaced the *irori* hearth as the centre of the living space).

Sashiko as embroidery, stitched before piecing the patchwork blocks, has later been lightly quilted with polyester wadding (batting) inside. The main patterns are the local *hitomezashi* designs. Snow on Mount Chōkai's twin peaks has been suggested with *hishizashi* (page 105) in straight lines. The border sashiko is stitched through all three quilt layers. *Seigaiha* (page 68) and *hiyoku igeta* (page 81) have been stitched in fine thread as part of the final quilting.

Tablecloth
contemporary work by Chieko Hori

The centre detail of this large tablecloth shows that sashiko doesn't have to be only light-coloured stitches on dark cloth. *Sanjū kakinohanazashi* (page 101) and the *yamagata* variation of *dan tsunagi* (page 74) frame the centre. Chieko says she imagined the shape of Mount Chōkai while stitching the borders. Several shades of indigo thread give variety to the central medallion, which has *hishizashi*, *futometsunagi* and *kasuri tsunagi* (pages 105 and 107) in squares on point, radiating outwards.

below: Chieko Hori (right) discussing sashiko designs with Reiko Domon (left) and Toshiko Takahashi, at her home in Yuza-machi, January 2002. A talented sashiko expert, sadly Chieko passed away shortly before this book was published. Her dream was sharing sashiko with people worldwide, in peace and friendship.

Acknowledgments

I would like to thank many people for their help and support in making this book a reality. First of all, a big 'domo arigato gozaimashita' to all my friends who have generously shared their time and work to help me with *The Ultimate Sashiko Sourcebook*. It would not have been possible without them.

Reiko Domon and Chie Ikeda for sashiko advice, information and organizing the 'Magic of Sashiko' teachers' group – Keiko Abe, Yukari Domon, Ryoko Kajiwara, Seiko Mimura, Aiko Sakuraba, Chitako Sato and Satoko Sato; everyone who kindly allowed me to feature their work in this book – Reiko Domon, Ayame Endo, Deborah Gordon, Chieko Hori, Keiko Hori, Chie Ikeda, Kiyoko Saito, Eiko Sasaki and Wendy Young; the Hori family, Domon family, Shibuya family and Sato family, who allowed me to photograph family heirlooms; special thanks to Chie Ikeda, Chieko Hori and Ayame Endo, whose work is shown in detail in the *hitomezashi* section.

Thanks to Mary and Shiro Tamakoshi (Euro Japan Links Limited) and Rie Tamakoshi for help with everything, especially the 'Magic of Sashiko' and keeping me supplied with materials; Hideo Abe of Yuza Town Office for arranging my New Year meeting with Mayor Ken Onedira and for helping with my sashiko research in Japan; Shōnai sashiko quilters past and present, especially Peaceful Heart Quilt Group and Hirata Town Sashiko Group, for inspiration; the Abe family, the Doi family, the Fukase Family and the Otaki family for their friendship and hospitality in Yamagata Prefecture; all my friends in Yuza-machi; my sashiko students; my friends and family, especially Guy who has had to live with a house full of sashiko; Val Shields and Mr Tanaka, who helped to display our sashiko exhibition; and finally my editors and all the team at David & Charles, for their patience with an ambitious project and my Japanese translations!

BIBLIOGRAPHY

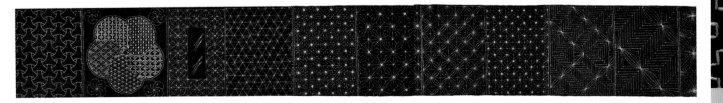

Arts of Japan 1 – Design Motifs, Saburo Mizoguichi (Shibundo, Tokyo/Weatherhill, New York, 1973)

Atarashii Sashiko, N. Seto (Nippon Vogue Co., Tokyo, 1998)

Beyond the Tanabata Bridge – Traditional Japanese Textiles, ed. William Jay Rathburn (Thames and Hudson/Seattle Art Museum, London, 1993)

The Clothes of the Ainu People, Kichiemon Okamura (Kyoto Shoin Co. Ltd, Kyoto, 1993)

The Compact Nelson Japanese-English Character Dictionary, Andrew Nelson (Charles E.Tuttle Co., Rutland/Tokyo, 1999)

Embroidery from Japan's Snow Country, Hiroko Ogawa, Threads (No.18) (The Taunton Press, Connecticut, 1988)

Geometric Patterns from Roman Mosaics, Robert Field (Tarquin Publications, Diss, 1999)

The Great Japan Exhibition – Art of the Edo Period 1600–1868, ed. William Watson (Royal Academy of Arts/ Weidenfeld and Nicolson, London, 1981)

An Illustrated Encyclopedia of Japanese Family Crests (Graphic-sha, Tokyo, 2001)

Japanese Costume and Textile Arts, Seiroku Noma (Heibonsha, Tokyo/Weatherhill, New York, 1974)

Japanese Country Quilting: Sashiko Patterns and Projects for Beginners, Karen Kim Matsunaga (Kodansha International, Tokyo, 1990)

Japanese Country Textiles, Anna Jackson (V&A Publications, London, 1997)

The Japanese-English Dictionary for Conversation about Japan, Jean Moore (Obunsha, Tokyo, 1989)

Japanese Fishermen's Coats from Awaji Island, Sharon Sadako Takaeda and Luke Roberts (UCLA Fowler Museum of Cultural History, Los Angeles, 2001)

Kimono – Fashioning Culture, Lisa Dalby (Vintage, London, 2001)

Kogin and Sashiko Stitch, Kiyoko Ogikubo (Kyoto Shoin Co. Ltd, Kyoto, 1993)

Mingei – Masterpieces of Japanese Folkcraft, Souori Yanagi et al. (Kodansha International, Tokyo, 1991)

New Concise Japanese-English Dictionary (Sainseido Co. Ltd, Tokyo, 1985)

Nippon no Monyo, Kazuo Kobayashi (Nippon Vogue Co., Tokyo, 1997)

Noragi to Sashiko no Sekai, Michiko Suzuki, Furui Nunoni ni Miserana Kurashi (Gakken, Tokyo, 2003)

Sashiko, Eiko Yoshida (Ondori Co., Tokyo 1993)

Sashiko Hyakuyo, Eiko Yoshida (Bunka Shuppan Kyoku, Tokyo, 1981)

Shonai Sashiko, Hirata Town Sashiko Group (Hirata Town Council, Yamagata, 1999)

Snow, Wave, Pine – Traditional Patterns in Japanese Design, Sadao Hibi & Motoji Niwa (Kodansha International, Tokyo, 2001)

Stitching Against the Cold: The Sashiko Emboidery of Aomori, Japan, Lynne Milgram, Piecework (Vol. II, no.5) (Interweave Press, Loveland, Colorado, 1994)

Out of the Blue: The Living Tradition of the Japanese Indigo Craft, Junco Sato Pollack, Piecework (Vol.II, no.5) (Interweave Press, Loveland, Colorado, 1994)

Traditional Japanese Small Motif, Kamon Yoshimoto (Page One Publishing, Singapore, 1993)

Tsutsugaki Textiles of Japan, Gensho Sasakura (Shikosha, Kyoto, 1987)

SUPPLIERS

UK

The Caron Collection
email: mail@caron-net.com
www.caron-net.com
*For hand-dyed and variegated
embroidery threads*

The Cotton Patch
1285 Stratford Road, Hall Green,
Birmingham, West Midlands B28 9AJ, UK
tel: 0121 7022840
email: mailorder@cottonpatch.net
www.cottonpatch.co.uk
*Quilter's rulers, fabric markers and
quilting supplies (webstore, mail order
and shop)*

Euro Japan Links Ltd
32 Nant Road, Childs Hill, London
NW2 2AT, UK
tel: 020 8201 9324
email: eurojpn@aol.com
www.eurojapanlink.co.uk
*Japanese textiles and sashiko supplies
(mail order only)*

Barbara Howell Something Special
Cae Cam, Ochr y Bryn, Henllan,
Denbighshire LL16 5AT, UK
*Hand-dyed threads and fabrics
(mail order only – send SAE)*

Oliver Twists
22 Phoenix Road, Crowther,
Washington, Tyne and Wear
NE38 0AD, UK
tel: 0191 416 6016
fax: 0191 4153405
email: jean@olivertwists.freeserve.co.uk
*Hand-dyed embroidery threads and
fabric (mail order and factory shop)*

Mulberry Silks
Silkwood, 4 Park Close, Tetbury,
Gloucestershire GL8 8HS, UK
tel: 01666 503438
www.mulberrysilks-patriciawood.com
*Raw silk, dupion and silk thread
(webstore and mail order)*

The Smithfield Gallery
Unit 9, Lake Enterprise Park, Caton
Road, Lancaster LA1 3NX, UK
tel: 01524 762 883
www.smithfieldgallery.co.uk
*Linen and other unusual fabrics
(webstore and mail order)*

FRANCE

Tissu Creatif
La Ville Guyomard, Laurenan 22230
France
tel: 33/296 25 7448
fax: 33/296 25 7448
*Checked, striped and plain cottons
(mail order only – write for information)*

USA

Joann Stores Inc
5555 Darrow Road, Hudson, Ohio, USA
tel: 1-888 739 4120
email: guestservice@jo-annstores.com
www.joann.com
*General needlework and quilting
supplies (mail order and stores
across the US)*

The Shibori Dragon
11124 Gravelly Lake Drive SW,
Lakewood WA 98499 USA
tel: (253) 582-7455 fax: (253) 512-2323
email: shiboridragon@juno.com
www.shiboridragon.com
*Japanese textiles and sashiko supplies
(webstore and mail order)*

AUSTRALIA

Abundia
PO Box 282, Paddington, QLD 4064,
Australia
tel/fax: (07) 33356 6508
email: orders@abundia.com
www.abundia.com
*Japanese textiles and sashiko supplies
(webstore and mail order)*

JAPAN
Sashiko supplies are sold in virtually
every handicraft or sewing store.

Chidori Antique Gallery, LLC
157–3 Zao Narisawa, Yamagata City
990–2334, Japan
email: gallery@chidori.com
tel/fax: 81-23-688-7933
www.chidori.com
*Vintage Japanese indigo fabric,
country clothing and sashiko
(webstore, mail order and shop)*

Kimono Flea Market Ichiroya
Asia-Shoji Bldg. 301, 1841-1 Nishi 1
Chome, Wakamatsu cho Tondabayashi,
Osaka 584-0025 Japan
email: info@ ichiroya.com
www.ichiroya.com
*Vintage textiles and sashiko
(webstore and mail order)*

Mi-Mu Club
1-3-15-405 Tomobuchi-cho, Miyakojima-
ku, Osaka, Japan
fax: 81-6-6921-9778
email: webmaster@mimuclub.com
www.mimuclub.com
*Japanese fabric and sashiko supplies
(webstore and mail order)*

SASHIKO PATTERN INDEX

Patterns are indexed by Japanese names, as some have various English translations. Where patterns have more than one name, all the common names are listed. *Moyōzashi* patterns are in **bold italics** and described on pages 58–95; *Hitomezashi* patterns are in *italics* and described on pages 96–109.

INDEX